MACMILLAN MODERN NOVELISTS
DORIS LESSING

Ruth Whittaker

MACMILLAN

First published 1988

Published by
Higher and Further Education Division
MACMILLAN PUBLISHERS LTD
Houndmills, Basingstoke, Hampshire RG21 2XS
and London
Companies and representatives
throughout the world

Typeset by Wessex Typesetters
(Division of The Eastern Press Ltd)
Frome, Somerset

Printed in China

British Library Cataloguing Publication Date
Whittaker, Ruth
Doris Lessing.—(Modern novelists).
1. Fiction in English. Lessing, Doris,
1919–. Critical studies
I. Title II. Series
823′.914
ISBN 0–333–40752–0
ISBN 0–333–40753–9 Pbk

MACMILLAN MODERN NOVELISTS

General Editor: Norman Page

MACMILLAN MODERN NOVELISTS

Published titles

ALBERT CAMUS Philip Thody
FYODOR DOSTOEVSKI Peter Conradi
E. M. FORSTER Norman Page
WILLIAM GOLDING James Gindin
GRAHAM GREENE Neil McEwan
HENRY JAMES Alan Bellringer
DORIS LESSING Ruth Whittaker
MARCEL PROUST Philip Thody
SIX WOMEN NOVELISTS Merryn Williams
JOHN UPDIKE Judie Newman
EVELYN WAUGH Jacqueline McDonnell
H. G. WELLS Michael Draper

Forthcoming titles

JOSEPH CONRAD Owen Knowles
WILLIAM FAULKNER David Dowling
F. SCOTT FITZGERALD John S. Whitley
GUSTAVE FLAUBERT David Roe
JAMES JOYCE Richard Brown
D. H. LAWRENCE G. M. Hyde
MALCOLM LOWRY Tony Bareham
GEORGE ORWELL Valerie Meyers
BARBARA PYM Michael Cotsell
PAUL SCOTT G. K. Das
MURIEL SPARK Norman Page
GERTRUDE STEIN Shirley Neuman
VIRGINIA WOOLF Edward Bishop

Series Standing Order

If you would like to receive future titles in this series as they are published, you can make use of our standing order facility. To place a standing order please contact your bookseller or, in case of difficulty, write to us at the address below with your name and address and the name of the series. Please state with which title you wish to begin your standing order. (If you live outside the UK we may not have the rights for your area, in which case we will forward your order to the publisher concerned.)

Standing Order Service, Macmillan Distribution Ltd, Houndmills, Basingstoke, Hampshire, RG21 2XS, England.

Contents

Acknowledgements

I am very grateful to Dr Mara Kalnins for her invaluable help in reading and commenting on the drafts of this book. I should also like to thank my husband, David Whittaker, for his assistance with the index, and for his great support and encouragement.

The author and publishers wish to thank the following who have kindly given permission for the use of copyright material:

Jonathan Cape Ltd for extracts from *The Summer Before the Dark, Re: Colonized Planet 5, Shikasta, The Marriages Between Zones Three, Four, and Five, The Sirian Experiments, The Making of the Representative for Planet 8, Documents Relating to the Sentimental Agents in the Volyen Empire* and *The Good Terrorist* by Doris Lessing; Grafton Books for extracts from *Martha Quest, A Proper Marriage, A Ripple from the Storm, Landlocked* and *The Four-Gated City* by Doris Lessing; Harper & Row for extracts from *The Grass is Singing*; Michael Joseph Ltd for extracts from *The Grass is Singing, Going Home, The Golden Notebook* and *The Diaries of Jane Somers* by Doris Lessing; Alfred A. Knopf, Inc. for extracts from *The Summer Before the Dark, The Memoirs of a Survivor, Shikasta, The Making of the Representative for Planet 8* and *The Four-Gated City* by Doris Leesing; Octagon Press Ltd for extracts from *The Memoirs of a Survivor* by Doris Lessing; Simon and Schuster, Inc. for extracts from *The Golden Notebook* and *Children of Violence – Martha Quest – Vol. 1* by Doris Lessing.

Every effort has been made to trace all the copyright holders but if any have inadvertently been overlooked the publishers will be pleased make the necessary arrangement at the first opportunity.

General Editor's Preface

The death of the novel has often been announced, and part of the secret of its obstinate vitality must be its capacity for growth, adaptation, self-renewal and even self-transformation: like some vigorous organism in a speeded-up Darwinian ecosystem, it adapts itself quickly to a changing world. War and revolution, economic crisis and social change, radically new ideologies such as Marxism and Freudianism, have made this century unprecedented in human history in the speed and extent of change, but the novel has shown an extraordinary capacity to find new forms and techniques and to accommodate new ideas and conceptions of human nature and human experience, and even to take up new positions on the nature of fiction itself.

In the generations immediately preceding and following 1914, the novel underwent a radical redefinition of its nature and possibilities. The present series of monographs is devoted to the novelists who created the modern novel and to those who, in their turn, either continued and extended, or reacted against and rejected, the traditions established during that period of intense exploration and experiment. It includes a number of those who lived and wrote in the nineteenth century but whose innovative contribution to the art of fiction makes it impossible to ignore them in any account of the origins of the modern novel; it also includes the so-called 'modernists' and those who in the mid and later twentieth century have emerged as outstanding practitioners of this genre. The scope is, inevitably, international; not only, in the migratory and exile-haunted world of our century, do writers refuse to heed national frontiers – 'English' literature lays claims to Conrad the Pole, Henry James the American, and Joyce the Irishman – but geniuses such as Flaubert, Dostoevski and Kafka have had an influence on the fiction of many nations.

Each volume in the series is intended to provide an introduction to the fiction of the writer concerned, both for those approaching him or her for the first time and for those who are already familiar with some parts of the achievement in question and now wish to place it in the context of the total *oeuvre*. Although essential information relating to the writer's life and times is given, usually in an opening chapter, the approach is primarily critical and the emphasis is not upon 'background' or generalisations but upon close examination of important texts. Where an author is notably prolific, major texts have been selected for detailed attention but an attempt has also been made to convey, more summarily, a sense of the nature and quality of the author's work as a whole. Those who want to read further will find suggestions in the select bibliography included in each volume. Many novelists are, of course, not only novelists but also poets, essayists, biographers, dramatists, travel writers and so forth; many have practised shorter forms of fiction; and many have written letters or kept diaries that constitute a significant part of their literary output. A brief study cannot hope to deal with all these in detail, but where the shorter fiction and the non-fictional writings, public and private, have an important relationship to the novels, some space has been devoted to them.

NORMAN PAGE

In joyous memory
of
Joan Bridge

1
Background and Influences

Doris Lessing was born in Persia in 1919, of British parents. Her father, Alfred Tayler, had fought in the First World War. He was badly wounded, and as a result of his injuries he had a leg amputated. He subsequently married Maud McVeigh, one of the nurses who had looked after him in hospital. After the war he went to work for the Imperial Bank of Persia in Tehran, but on leave in 1925 he went to the Empire Exhibition in London and was attracted to the idea of farming in Southern Rhodesia. On impulse he went to Africa the same year, taking his wife and two young children, and bought three thousand acres of land with a government loan.

Doris and her younger brother Harry were brought up on an isolated farm where their father made a very meagre living growing maize and tobacco. Both children went to boarding schools. Doris attended a Catholic convent in Salisbury, followed by a year at a state school. She finished her formal education at the age of 14, deliberately thwarting her parents' academic ambitions for her, but continued to educate herself by reading very widely. She began her working life in Salisbury at a telephone company and later, having learnt typewriting and shorthand, worked first as a legal secretary, and then as a Hansard secretary in the Rhodesian parliament.

In Salisbury Doris Tayler led the lively social life of a young, unmarried white girl in the 1930s. She met a civil servant called Frank Wisdom whom she married in 1939. They had two children, John and Jean, but the marriage ended in divorce in 1943. During the war Doris became increasingly interested in politics, and she joined a small Marxist group where she met a half-Jewish German refugee called Gottfried Lessing, who she married in 1945. Their son Peter was born in 1947, and they divorced in 1949. Mrs Lessing has not remarried, and has said:

1

'I do not think marriage is one of my talents. I've been happier unmarried than married.'[1]

In 1949 she came to London, bringing her son and the manuscript of her first novel, *The Grass is Singing*. This was accepted by Michael Joseph, the first publisher she approached, and was an immediate success when it was published in 1950. She has remained in England ever since, although she has travelled widely. She is reticent about her private life, and interviews over the years have been confined mainly to discussions about her work.

Doris Lessing's background has been a powerful influence on her fiction. She has written, 'we use our parents like recurring dreams, to be entered into when needed. They are always there for love or hate.'[2] She has described her father as 'not living in the real world' and her mother as 'brave and resourceful'[3] but her sympathies clearly lie with her father. Her parents have made their mark on her work, not only in her characterisation of them in her novels, but also in that the clash of their personalities seems to have been a motivating force behind her compulsion to become a writer in the first place. As Lorna Sage points out,[4] the roles of Doris Lessing's parents echo those of Olive Schreiner, a writer she greatly admired. In an Afterword to Olive Schreiner's novel *The Story of An African Farm* (1885) Doris Lessing writes:

> To the creation of a woman novelist seem to go certain psychological ingredients; at least, often enough to make it interesting. One of them, a balance between father and mother where the practicality, the ordinary sense, cleverness, and worldly ambition is on the side of the mother; and the father's life is so weighted with dreams and ideas and imaginings that their joint life gets lost in what looks like a hopeless muddle and failure, but which holds a potentiality for something that must be recognized as better, on a different level, than what ordinary sense or cleverness can begin to conceive.[5]

This 'potentiality' was not realised by Doris Lessing's parents, but is somehow taken on by her. It is as if their poverty, their unconventionality, their resigned irritation with their lot, acted as an abrasive stimulus for their daughter to continue the struggle to make sense of, or vindicate, her father's unworldliness, to ratify the worth of his dreams. She does this, locally but specifically, when she dedicates *Canopus in Argos: Archives* to him, long after his death: 'For my father, who used to sit, hour after hour, night after night, outside our house in Africa, watching the stars. "Well," he would say, "if we blow ourselves up, there's plenty more where we came from!"' Alfred Tayler's wild ideas blazed recurrently throughout Doris's youth: gold-divining, strange scientific experiments, eccentric political theories. Against the hard, practical necessity of making a success of the farm, these must have seemed infuriatingly irrelevant. Nevertheless, his daughter sympathised with his turn of mind, and her work has from the start combined 'practicality . . . sense, cleverness' with 'dreams and ideas and imaginings', and ultimately it is the non-rational which is seen as a source of hope and salvation.

Doris Lessing's literary career spans nearly forty years, and during that time her focus has shifted. Critical attempts to pin her down and label her as 'Marxist', 'feminist' or, more recently, a 'mystic', have been superseded by the evolution of her ideas. It is almost as if by the time she comes to write a novel she has already moved on from the ideological force which motivated it. In that way, in a personal sense, her work is always retrospective, rather than exploratory. It does not seem so, however, because like a highly sensitive cosmic seismograph, she has a striking ability to detect cultural shifts in the universal consciousness before they are actually manifest. This makes her work seem at first prophetic, then emblematic of the society she describes, and there is often a time lapse between publication of her novels and a recognition of them as saying something generally applicable. For example, she wrote about the problems of apartheid before it was in the forefront of people's minds; *The Golden Notebook* (1962) represented the thoughts and feelings of women long before it was understood to be representative; her holistic approach to madness and dreams was in advance of what is now widely accepted; her warnings about the likelihood of a nuclear holocaust are still not taken seriously by the majority of the population. She herself is always impatient to move on, and aware that her views will soon seem to her not inaccurate but outdated. In an interview with Florence Howe she says: 'In five years time, I'll be saying, my god, what a fool

I was. I really do feel this way about every two years – what a fool I was two years ago.'[6] It would seem indeed that Doris Lessing's principal interest lies not in any specific ideology, or empirical truths about any section of society, but in the nature of change itself. In 1969 she said: 'What interests me more than anything is how our minds are changing, how our ways of perceiving reality are changing.'[7] And this is reiterated in 1982 in the Afterword to *The Making of the Representative for Planet 8*, where she says:

> I think there must be definite lifespans for ideas or sets of related ideas. They are born (or reborn), come to maturity, decay, die, are replaced. If we do not at least ask ourselves if this is in fact a process, if we do not make the attempt to treat the mechanisms of ideas as something we may study, with impartiality, what hope have we of controlling them? (p. 170)

So, although certain themes recur in Mrs Lessing's novels, her emphasis is given to them in the knowledge that her commitment to them is provisional, and she conveys this to her readers. These themes include colonialism, politics, the roles of women in relation to men and to each other, the purposes of madness, dreams and prophecy, the nature of art and the purposes of education.

The concept of colonialism is important to Doris Lessing's work. It applies not only to the African settings of some of her novels and short stories, but also to her way of seeing. For her there are two Africas: the country which has always belonged to the African, and the veneer the white colonial has imposed upon it. She belongs to neither in any real sense, and it is this marginality which enables her to act as an observer, and gives an additional clarity to that detachment which is an essential prerequisite of the artist. In 1949, when she went to London, which was more nearly her home in cultural terms, she was still an outsider, and saw it as a strange country. This lends great power to her descriptions of the blitzed buildings, and of the natives and their tribal habits. Her non-fiction work, *In Pursuit of the English* (1960) draws on her early days in England, material which is fictionalised at the beginning of *The Four-Gated City* (1969). She was not able to use the shorthand available to a British-born writer, based on the knowledge of common assumptions between writer and reader. Her colonial, expatriate eye makes strange the familiar, and her readers are thus reintroduced to what they thought they already knew, from a different perspective. In her later fiction she is perfectly able to view this planet from afar since she has always stood at a distance from her material. Perhaps it is not surprising that in her series of science fiction novels, *Canopus in Argos: Archives*, she posits a system of a galactic colonialism (albeit a seemingly benign one) because she herself is an oecist. Her own sense of displacement, of not belonging, enables her to work on the borders of our consciousness: charting, mapping, delineating an unknown country, acting in fact like a new colonial, pioneering and appropriating new territory.

Mrs Lessing's political views were a further means of distancing herself from her material, of viewing her society from the outside. During the Second World War she joined a communist group in Rhodesia, which she saw as a way of fighting apartheid. She read a great deal of Marxist theory, but was quick to perceive the gap between theory and practice, a situation she exploits with some irony in *A Ripple from the Storm* (1958). She seems to have been attracted to the people who comprised the Marxist group because, unlike the hearty, sports-playing colonials in Salisbury, they were intellectuals interested in effecting social change. Such people were rare in Rhodesia at that time, and the group, with its wartime influx of British airmen and European refugees, provided Doris Lessing with her higher education. The group was very isolated in the prevailing social and cultural climate, although they became slightly more acceptable after Russia became a British ally in 1941. Although her commitment to Communist Party doctrine was less than whole-hearted, what she liked about Marxism was its unifying vision. In the 1971 Preface to *The Golden Notebook* she says:

Marxism looks at things as a whole and in relation to each other — or tries to. . . . A person who has been influenced by Marxism takes it for granted that an event in Siberia will affect one in Botswana. I think it is possible that Marxism was the first attempt, for our time, outside the formal religions, at a world-mind, a world ethic. (pp. 14–15)

This idea of unity is a powerful dynamic in Mrs Lessing's work. Each novel is part of her research into how it can be achieved, and potential solutions such as Marxism, feminism, mysticism are examined within her fiction. But the examination often reveals limitations and inconsistencies. One of the dilemmas for the artist who is also a Marxist is the question of subjectivity. The person who writes from personal commitment instead of being at the service of the party is liable to criticism. In an article called 'A Small Personal Voice' published in 1957, Mrs Lessing mentions a visit to Moscow she made in 1952 where in conversation with her a writer spoke, not of crude political pressures on him, but of an 'inner censor' which ensured that what he wrote was politically acceptable. She deplores this, and in *The Golden Notebook* examines a similar dilemma. The heroine, a novelist, suffers from writer's 'block' because she feels guilt at writing about personal emotions rather than about the revolutionary struggles going on all over the world. In the Preface Mrs Lessing explains how she solved this for herself:

The way to deal with the problem of 'subjectivity', that shocking business of being preoccupied with the tiny individual who is at the same time caught up in an explosion of terrible and marvellous possibilities, is to see him as a microcosm and in this way to break through the personal, the subjective, making the personal general, as indeed life always does, transforming a private experience – or so you think of it when still a child, '*I* am falling in love', '*I* am feeling this or that emotion, or thinking that or the other thought' – into something much larger: growing up is after all only the understanding that one's unique and incredible experience is what everyone shares. (pp. 13–14)

What is most personal is also most universal, and thus the charge of individualism is refuted.

Mrs Lessing seems to have had little political involvement during her first few years in England, but in 1952 she visited the Soviet Union, and from 1952–3 helped Margot Heinemann edit a magazine called *Daylight* for the encouragement of working-class writers. She was later associated with a Marxist magazine called the *New Reasoner*, a journal founded outside the official Communist Party, in which some of her short stories first appeared. In the late 1950s Doris Lessing was one of the founder members of the Campaign for Nuclear Disarmament, and helped to organise the first Aldermaston march protesting against nuclear weapons. In 1956 she published a socialist realist novel called *Retreat to Innocence*, the only one of her novels which can be described as overtly propagandist. In the same year Khrushchev denounced Stalin at the Twentieth Congress of the Russian Communist Party, but invaded Hungary later in the same year. Doris Lessing resigned from the Communist Party, and in an additional note at the end of *Going Home* written early in 1957 she says: 'In this book I have made various statements about the possibility of Communism becoming democratic. Since writing it, the Soviet intervention in Hungary has occurred' (p. 297). In *A Ripple from the Storm* (1958) she demonstrates not so much her disillusion with Marxism but rather her growing certainty that its rhetoric was far removed from its effectiveness as a political force. Nevertheless, in 1967 she says 'the communist countries, save for China, have all become much more democratic' ('Eleven Years Later': *Going Home*, 1968 edition). In 1982 she writes a further postscript, and is appalled by her earlier views:

> I have been forced to read . . . the record of my changes of mind about communism. Embarrassing. I would prefer not to have them exposed, because like others of my kind, the former reds, I wonder how it was possible that I held such views. . . . I said as late as 1967 that I believed the communist countries were getting more democratic. *I did?* I did. How could I have conceivably believed such nonsense? (Postscript: *Going Home*, 1982 edition).

The Four-Gated City (1969) captures very vividly the atmosphere of communist and left-wing circles in Britain in the 1950s, the feelings of disillusion and betrayal. Political rhetoric is attacked in *Canopus in Argos: Archives* and by the time she comes to write *The Good Terrorist* (1985) she is openly satirical about the ways in which jargon is used indiscriminately as a substitute for thought-out opinions. In her book about the Russian invasion of Afghanistan, *The Wind Blows Away our Words*, Doris Lessing is both anti-Russian and anti-communist. The dominant tone of the book, however, is not so much anger at the Russians, as a kind of exasperated despair with the West for its impervious attitude to the Afghans' suffering.'

Perhaps the most lasting legacy of Mrs Lessing's political commitment is not the content of her novels, but her dialectical method of working. Instead of accepting her raw material, as it were, and trying to make sense of it, she puts up its antithesis; the resulting creative clash makes a new synthesis. Thus apartheid, ideologically opposed, is shown in all its tragic potential; motherhood and domesticity, instead of being ratified, are countered and challenged, and the woman grows. In *The Golden Notebook*, instead of ordering her material realistically, Doris Lessing sets it in contrast to her own fragmented vision, and the seeming impossibility of any kind of completeness. Thus it becomes an epistemological novel, not as the result of a deliberate philosophical intent, but through the dialectical process of confronting its realism with its intrinsic contradictions – the formal conventions and devices inherent in a work of art.

Since the mid 1960s Mrs Lessing has been regarded as one of the early voices of the feminist movement, and *The Golden Notebook* one of its key texts. In the 1971 preface she rejected this view: 'this novel was not a trumpet for Women's Liberation', and goes on to say that it 'was written as if the attitudes that have been created by the Women's Liberation movements already existed' (p. 9). More recent criticism has agreed with Doris Lessing's denial of *The Golden Notebook* as a feminist text, although for different reasons. For example, Elizabeth Wilson writes:

. . . in some ways what Doris Lessing says is the antithesis of women's liberation. The situation and consciousness of her fractured heroine, Anna, is precisely the situation and consciousness the feminists of the late 1960s were in revolt *against*. They were trying *not* to feel bounded within masculine sexuality. They were trying to find a voice in politics, to live politics, to take women into the political arena instead of rejecting the political arena as an ultimate falsification.[8]

So the pendulum swings from the lack of feminist response to the novel on its publication in 1962 (since the climate for such a response did not then exist), to its adoption as a central text of the Women's Movement, and now to its rejection by feminists as an inadequate statement of their cause. These swings simply emphasise a social and critical evolution; they do not undermine the fact that in her novels Doris Lessing has always been concerned with the condition of women, even if her thoughts do not always coincide with those of the feminist movement over the last twenty years. Indeed, it is possible to see women's search for identity as a crucial theme in Doris Lessing's work. Not a corporate identity, however, but personal identities painfully sought out and worked for through the gradual shedding of masks, disguises, roles, attitudes and customs.

Doris Lessing consistently refuses to follow a prescribed line, or to become a spokesperson for any kind of movement. Some of her heroines' aims, such as their desire for selves separate from roles as daughters, wives, mistresses and mothers, reflect those emphasised in feminist polemics. But other aims, such as their tenacious searches for possible, good relationships with men, do not. During a tour of North America in 1984 Mrs Lessing was taken to task for her 'betrayal' of the feminist cause. She was unrepentant, and said that 'women's politics are exactly like men's politics', and regretted that women have not co-operated with men to solve problems common to them both: 'a great opportunity has been missed'.[9]

The truth is that she has never been a feminist, so that accusations of betrayal are irrelevant. Rather, she is a woman novelist whose antennae sensed the crucial issues of feminism and wrote about them long before they were common currency. Both Martha Quest in *The Children of Violence* and Anna Wulf in *The Golden Notebook* made shockingly articulate the desires and frustrations of women in the mid-twentieth century, and also offered some ways of working through them and finding solutions. In later novels such as *The Summer Before the Dark* (1973), *The Memoirs of a Survivor* (1974) and *The Marriages Between Zones Three, Four and Five* (1980) we are shown in detail the making, unmaking and remaking of the female heroines. That is to say that in each case the woman is shown to disintegrate, and to reintegrate into another mode of existence.

In *The Diaries of Jane Somers* and *The Good Terrorist* Mrs Lessing seems to be reworking the theme, almost as if she feels we have not yet absorbed the lessons of her earlier novels.

At one stage in her life Doris Lessing embarked on a period of psychotherapy with a Jungian therapist, and the influence of Jung's ideas shows in her fiction. Particularly important to her work is his concept of 'individuation', the process by which an individual works towards 'wholeness' through acknowledgement and incorporation of the different aspects of personality. All Mrs Lessing's novels are concerned with this process (and one could say are a record of *her* progress), although by the time she writes *Canopus in Argos: Archives* her emphasis changes. Throughout *Children of Violence* Martha Quest is aware of the disparate and incompatible elements of her character, and the novels describe her progress towards self-knowledge and transformation. Other novels, such as *The Golden Notebook*, *Briefing for a Descent into Hell*, *The Summer Before the Dark* and *The Memoirs of a Survivor* make the spiritual growth of their protagonists the main theme. To achieve this state of psychological unity, it is necessary to recognise the elements of both the conscious and the unconscious mind. In the latter, these are often the repressed tendencies, which Jung called 'shadow' and which are usually the negative and unpleasant aspects of the personality. This idea is crucial to an understanding of Doris Lessing's characters. From *The Grass is Singing* onwards, her heroines have to face aspects of themselves that they have formerly denied, for example, Mary Turner's sexuality, Martha Quest's 'self-hater', Anna Wulf's 'joy-in-destruction'. Often the pivot of the narrative is at such a moment of revelation. This acknowledgement of shadow is usually a liberating process, since it allows the person to be less than perfect, and to reclaim the energies used in maintaining a facade.

In addition to the personal unconscious, Jung also believed in what he called the 'collective unconscious', consisting of primordial images which recur as motifs throughout myths, dreams, fantasies and fairy tales. He called these 'archetypes', and they can take the form of, for example, a wise old man, a mother-figure, a seafarer, a trickster or a child. He also laid great stress on the circle as a symbol of unity, and when Doris Lessing mentions mandalas in her work she gives them a similar significance. In the same way, the four-gated city of Martha's vision in *Children of Violence* is an eloquent imaginative structure, because for Jung quaternity was symbolic of wholeness and harmony. In her fiction Mrs Lessing draws heavily on mythic patterns such as The Golden Age, the Fall and rebirth, and an understanding of her work depends on our awareness of this framework. She has said: 'All the metaphors I ever use are always extremely hoary on purpose. . . . When I wrote *The Memoirs of a Survivor* I deliberately chose all the most ancient images I could find like "the door", "the wall" . . . I think there can't be anything wrong with images that have been in use for thousands of years.'[10]

Archetypal figures frequently appear in dreams, which Jung regarded as highly important. For him dreams were a source of communication from the unconscious; a regulating and complementary balance to the conscious mind, often dealing with areas of the psyche which are unrealised or neglected. Doris Lessing frequently reveals material from the unconscious minds of her characters through visions, sexual ecstasy, sudden irrational thoughts, or dreams. Her use of dreams in her novels is extensive, and within them Jungian symbols occur, so that the reader is made aware of the characters' hidden desires, motivations and potentialities. In the *Children of Violence* series Martha's dreams are very significant, often giving her solutions to problems which have remained unsolved by conscious thought and worry. In *The Golden Notebook* Anna Wulf learns about herself through a careful scrutiny of her dreams. In *The Summer before the Dark* the dream sequence insistently teaches Kate Brown to listen to its promptings, and to take her direction from them.

Individuation entails separation from a group, and Jung makes clear that the changes wrought by crowd psychology are less long-lasting than those achieved by an individual. Martha Quest joins and then leaves groups, realising eventually that the prevailing mores and ideologies cannot accommodate her psychical growth. The social circle of young white colonials, the political groups in Africa and later in London are initially tempting, but soon restricting. Both Martha and Anna have to learn to separate themselves from movements and organisations that claim to speak for them; to remain loyal to a group means that compromises must be made which restrict personal

development. Jung believed that change in the collective begins
first by change in the individual, and in Doris Lessing's work
this is reinforced by the experience of her protagonists.

Jung attached great importance to the non-rational, and in
Mrs Lessing's novels and short stories breakdown and madness
are seen as states of great potential. Her views on madness are
very close to those of R. D. Laing, who sees so-called 'madness' as
a normal reaction to the fragmented state of the world, and also
that it may be the beginning of self-healing. In Doris Lessing's
first novel, *The Grass is Singing*, madness does lead literally to
death for the heroine, Mary Turner. For later protagonists,
such as Anna Wulf, Martha Quest and Charles Watkins, it is
an opportunity to confront the most feared and hated aspects of
the self, and to achieve a healing unity. Doris Lessing insists on
the need for her characters to undergo this experience, this
facing of evil, in order that they are presented with another
perspective on themselves, and on the world. In her novels, the
point of crisis is never simply negative. It carries simultaneously
the potential for change, which is often not perceived while
things are ostensibly going smoothly for the protagonists. This
is not to say that the process is without pain. Many of Doris
Lessing's characters suffer appallingly while confronting the
devils that have been conjured up, a suffering which is
intensified by the attitude of the 'sane' world to those it classifies
as 'mad'. Lynda, in *The Four-Gated City*, learns with difficulty to
cope with her inner world and the world outside, and eventually
grows skilful in holding on to her psychic gifts while managing
to maintain, sometimes tenuously, a link with everyday reality.
She gives Martha the confidence to experience madness, to
allow the full force of the non-rational to envelop her, and to
benefit from it. In Doris Lessing's fiction madness is not a state
leading nowhere, but a dynamic process usually leading to
change and a healing reconciliation within the person who
undergoes it. In this she strongly echoes Jung and Laing, both
of whom have undoubtedly had a powerful influence on her
work.

Because Mrs Lessing's viewpoint is continually evolving, she
shrugs off earlier influences, or rather, she incorporates them,
and moves on. For this reason she tends to resent critics who
emphasise her former allegiances, and in the early 1960s when

she began to be a student of the Sufi religion she looked back
on Jung as part of a much wider philosophy. She has said:

> I think Jung's views are good as far as they go, but he took
> them from Eastern philosophers who go much further. Ibn El
> Arabi and El Ghazzali, in the middle ages, had more
> developed ideas about the 'unconscious', collective or
> otherwise, than Jung, among others. He was a limited man.
> But useful as far as he went.[11]

Similarly she is irritated by suggestions that she has been
strongly influenced by R. D. Laing. When Roberta Rubenstein
suggested strong parallels between a case described in Laing's
book *The Politics of Experience* and Doris Lessing's book *Briefing
for a Descent into Hell*, she fought back: 'I had not taken Laing as
my starting point. I had not read the piece in question by
him. . . . My book was written out of my own thoughts, not
other people's.'[12] Other critics have made the same comparison,
and later Doris Lessing explained to Roberta Rubenstein that if
she sounded cross 'it was because I've had Laing too much. . . .
It's been my experience again and again . . . that you only have
to write something and what you write starts coming true in all
kinds of direct and indirect ways. It is as if you bring something
towards you if you imagine it and then write it.'[13] This prophetic
tone of her writing is one of her most startling and original
qualities. It is also extremely alarming in view of her pessimism
about the fate of this planet, which in *The Four-Gated City* and
later novels she sees as partially destroyed by nuclear war.

This terrifying vision gives an urgency to her work, and an
impetus to seek out and share a means of survival. In the Sufi
religion it would seem that she may have found an answer. Sufi
manifests itself variously in different centuries and cultures, and
one of its central notions is the evolutionary capacity of
mankind. Idries Shah, a contemporary teacher of Sufi who
numbers Mrs Lessing among his students, says:

> Sufis believe that, expressed in one way, humanity is evolving
> to a certain destiny. We are all taking part in that evolution.
> Organs come into being as a result of a need. . . . What
> ordinary people regard as sporadic and occasional bursts of

telepathic and prophetic power are seen by the Sufi as nothing less than the first stirrings of these same organs. . . . So essential is this rarefied evolution that our future depends on it.[14]

Doris Lessing quotes this passage in full in *The Four-Gated City* and this belief in the necessary cultivation of transcendent powers is an important aspect of her work from *Landlocked* onwards. The emphasis varies: sometimes it is more explicit than others. But her later novels delineate characters whose psychical growth begins from a conscious recognition of need, an awareness of something important just out of reach, almost inaudible. The idea of transcendence by various methods, and the urgency of its necessity in the face of a possible future holocaust, underlies her writing.

Another tenet of Sufi is the relative unimportance of the intellect and the processes of logical thought, compared with the value of understanding intuitively or through experience. The Sufi teaching story is therefore a method used to dislocate the listener's rational mind from its ordinary responses (in a similar way to the Zen koan 'What is the sound of one hand clapping?'). This kind of intuitive perception is familiar to Doris Lessing, who realises that experiences even of extra-sensory perception are actually quite common:

> You can see someone pick up what you are thinking and start talking about it. It happens to everybody. . . . Or you will say something and someone will say that's funny I've been thinking about that. In actual fact what we are doing is using ESP. . . . What energy is reaching you? We don't know why, do we? There is something there to be explored . . . if we don't get upset.[15]

Mrs Lessing is not upset about exploring the potentialities of ESP, but rather at what she sees as the limitations of conventional methods of acquiring knowledge. In her novels she castigates educational methods that rigidly exclude this kind of exploration, and it is possible to see *The Four-Gated City* as a cry of frustration with Western thought processes. When Martha begins to read esoteric literature she is appalled that 'her education, the education of everyone of her generation (and of how many generations back?) had been so set, so programmed, that not a word of this information had been able to come through to her except in odd fragments, phrases, notions, each one soaked in, redolent of, "dottiness", "eccentricity", shadiness, unpleasantness' (*The Four-Gated City*, p. 530). This would seem to be one of the reasons why Doris Lessing turned to space fiction as a medium for *Canopus in Argos: Archives*. She has long defended science fiction because it has so often been the imaginative precursor of scientific facts. But it also enables outrageous theories to be put forward in a format which renders them harmless; the licensed peculiarity of science fiction allows her to propound ideas that would be less acceptable in the confines of the traditional novel. In addition, by moving 'out of this world', it becomes much easier for a writer to describe spiritual aspiration or non-worldly states of being.

One of the problems that Doris Lessing's work presents is her great personal commitment to the issues she writes about. This means that, for example, her pessimism about the fate of this planet and her belief in the capacity of the human race to develop paranormal powers are not simply imaginative literary themes, but deeply held beliefs. And probably at least part of our response to Mrs Lessing's fiction depends on whether or not we share these beliefs. In addition, they entail a language which she has admitted is embarrassing and can cause ripples of self-consciousness. A vocabulary adequate to describe Mrs Lessing's work has to rely quite heavily on words such as 'unconscious', 'psychical' and 'transcendent'. A further problem is that she is not concerned to admit the difficulty of her concepts by adopting a rhetoric of persuasion. She writes from the standpoints of her evolving beliefs, and does not try to cajole the reader into an acceptance of them.

In view of her dislike of categorisations, it is perhaps appropriate that Doris Lessing's work is resistant to neat pigeon-holing. This study concentrates on her novels, the publication of which has been interspersed with short stories, plays and works of non-fiction. As some critics have noted,[16] her short stories are often rehearsals or exercises for her novels, so that there are similarities between, for example, the short story 'The Temptation of Jack Orkney' and the novel *Briefing for a*

Descent into Hell; between 'A Room' and *The Memoirs of a Survivor*; between 'To Room 19' and *The Summer Before the Dark*; between 'An Old Woman and her Cat' and *The Diary of a Good Neighbour*. Doris Lessing's two plays, *Each His Own Wilderness* (1959) and *Play with a Tiger* (1962) both use material which echoes episodes in *The Golden Notebook*. Indeed, in that novel Anna says 'I must write a play about Anna and Saul and the tiger' (p. 593). So throughout her work there is a creative interweaving, a free interaction between themes and genres which subverts a logical, progressive critical explication – a fact which would delight her. Even if we avoid the obvious traps of describing her as an ex-Marxist, an unwilling feminist or a reluctant seer, there is still the temptation to give a spurious cohesion to her fiction, to suggest that she moves steadily from realism to fabulation, as if one excluded the other. But this will not do, because her work is far less linear than this suggests. Her realism has always been irradiated with the visionary, from her first novel. She dislikes the either/or format, and in her novels she inveighs against the set of mind that cannot admit contradictions, inconsistencies, grey areas and ambiguity. Her novels deal both with the reality of everyday life, and with the complementary aspects of the unconscious mind, often ahead of rational thought. This poses problems for most of us who think in terms of reality or fantasy, realism or fabulation, sanity or madness, real life or dreams. But in *Briefing for a Descent into Hell* the protagonist gives us some help. He says 'It is not *or*, that is the point. It is *and*. Everything is. Your dreams *and* your life' (p. 142). And that is a good starting point from which to approach Doris Lessing's novels.

2
The Colonial Legacy

Southern Rhodesia (now Zimbabwe) was Doris Lessing's home for twenty-five years, and her feeling for Africa has deeply influenced her work. In *Going Home* (1957) she describes the house she lived in as a child. It was a 'pole-and-dagga' house, made of indigenous materials: a skeleton of wooden poles, mud walls, earth floor and a thatch of wild grasses. The walls were uneven, the roof leaked, and every year during the wet season a young tree grew up through the floor. When, after twenty years, her parents left the house, it became overrun with antheaps and then by fire, and subsided back into the bush. But it remained 'home' in Doris Lessing's imagination. She writes: 'I worked out recently that I have lived in over sixty houses, flats and rented rooms during the past twenty years and not in one of them have I felt at home. . . . The fact is, I don't live anywhere; I never have since I left that first house on the kopje' (*Going Home*, p. 37). The primitive nature of the house, the unceasing war against destructive ants and insects, the talk of the adults on the veranda, the sense of space and isolation – all these were potent factors in Doris Lessing's childhood. After seven years in England she returned to Southern Rhodesia for a visit in 1956, an emotional necessity. She writes about driving out of the town into the bush, only five minutes away:

And now for the first time I was really home. The night was magnificent; the Southern Cross on a slant overhead; the moon a clear, small pewter; the stars all recognizable and close. The long grass stood all around, tall and giving off its dry, sweetish smell, and full of talking crickets. The flattened trees of the highveld were low above the grass, low and a dull silver-green. . . . if I had had to fly back to England the next

17

day, I would have been given what I had gone home for.
(*Going Home*, p. 38)

Mrs Lessing may have returned home to try to recapture a
sense of her childhood and of belonging. Nevertheless, hers is a
colonial heritage, and carries with it the sense of not belonging.
To be a colonial means essentially that one is living in a strange
land, and this applies even when the colonial's family has lived
for generations in a foreign country. Of course it is 'home'. But
it is also alien, a place of deep cultural differences, which means
that the settlers cannot be at one with the country they have
adopted. In order to maintain what they feel to be their
separateness and their identity, they carry their own cultural
distinctiveness in their heads and in their hearts, imposing it
where it can be imposed, distancing themselves from areas
where it cannot be.

A way of coming to terms with the 'new' country is the
manufacture of myths by which I mean the invention of false
lore as a coping mechanism. Indeed, this process of mythopoeia
seems an integral part of the psychology of colonialism. As in
the American West or Australasia, frontier myths, settler myths,
were adapted to fit the circumstances of the country. In the
colonial experience, myths replace history which contains
inconvenient facts, such as the Great Zimbabwe ruins of an
earlier culture. They are cultivated, for example, in order to
justify the white takeover of Africa, and to maintain the whites'
assumption of their superiority to the black populations. Thus,
the most powerful myths were those which emphasised the
white 'rescue' of the country from savagery, and the 'civilising'
influence of a European culture. Cecil Rhodes was seen as a
great pioneer, taking over an empty land. As Anthony Chennells
points out,[17] the myth of the uncreated land harks back to the
mythology of a Golden Age, but with the irresistible advantage
of the possibility of making it a contemporary experience. In
fact, this part of Africa was quite heavily populated in the late
nineteenth century, and the native black peoples were moved to
reserves or killed to make room for the white farmers. Doris
Lessing describes this displacement and its effect on the land
and both white and black peoples in her story 'The Old Chief
Mshlanga'. At the end of the story the white man's cook, son of
a tribal chief, translates for his father: 'My father says: All this

land, this land you call yours, is his land, and belongs to our people' (*Collected African Stories*, vol I, p. 24). In a review of *Out of Africa* by Karen Blixen, Mrs Lessing says 'she never saw that her 6,000 acres were not hers.'[18] Throughout her work she acknowledges the Africans' right to Africa, and deplores the average white colonialist's ignorance of their complex tribal history and culture, threatened with destruction. Nevertheless, there is some ambiguity in her attitude, since in her short stories and in her non-fictional writings about the country of her upbringing, Doris Lessing often gives us a strong impression that it is *her* Africa she is writing about. This dichotomy is expressed in *Going Home*: 'Africa belongs to the Africans; the sooner they take it back the better. But – a country also belongs to those who feel at home in it' (Ch. 1). And she too is drawn to the myth of the empty, uncreated Africa. In *Going Home* she writes of 'its emptiness, its promise' and says: 'It is still uncreated. . . . Because it is so empty we can dream. We can dream of cities and of a civilisation more beautiful than anything that has been seen in the world before' (Ch. 1). The very space of Africa lends itself to the vision of the Four-Gated City – not a usurpation by the whites, but an ideal, multi-racial community living in harmony and peace, a reconciliation.

A further colonial myth was the egalitarianism of the white settlers. Having in common the colour of their skins, they strove to show a united front to the black population, a situation explored by Doris Lessing in *The Grass is Singing* (1950), where white solidarity is depicted straining to breaking point. In the *Children of Violence* sequence we are shown that in fact the white Rhodesians were aware of a wide variety of classes amongst themselves. They were anxious to distinguish themselves from the Afrikaners, but the resulting cohesion was not without its contradictions. When the RAF airmen arrived during the Second World War, they were regarded as socially inferior to the officers, some of whom, in turn, looked down on the colony as bourgeois and provincial. Perhaps the most powerful (and the most necessary) myth was that of the unbridgeable gap between the black and white races. By the 1930s and 1940s the maintenance of white superiority was becoming increasingly difficult to justify in economic and political terms: poor whites and educated blacks muddled the simplicity of earlier categorisations. Thus the need to believe in the gulf became even stronger, and the black man was resolutely viewed as an ignorant savage so that the contrast with the enlightened, civilising white man could be more clearly emphasised.

Sexual relations between the races were a powerful challenge to their separateness; here, a double standard prevailed. Miscegenation between white men and black women is shown to be tolerated, although not generally approved. Sexual relations between white women and black men were unthinkable, although if brought to the conscious consideration of white society, rape, one assumes, would have been preferable to willing acquiescence. That the idea of a white woman actually being attracted to a black man was considered so shocking, perhaps reveals the prevalence of such an unconscious desire, and much of the power of *The Grass is Singing* comes from the way Doris Lessing analyses this taboo.

Everywhere in Mrs Lessing's work, myths collide with real life. Many of her short stories have for their main theme the clash of cultures where the colonial myths do not suffice to protect their perpetrators from African reality. Indeed, much of her writing focuses on that precise point where her characters are confronted with the inadequacy of their sustaining fantasies. What we are shown is the drama where a façade breaks down, or where a cultural reversal takes place: a native herbal medicine saves a white child's sight; a white woman feels sexual desire for a black servant; the white father of an illegitimate black boy agrees to send him to university; a farmer or his wife is defeated by loneliness; a white boy begins to understand the uncompromising nature of the veld. There is drama inherent in the colonial situation, because the alien country and its native occupants are antagonists of the colonial, at least implicitly. From G. A. Henty to Doris Lessing the narrative suspense (who will win?) does not have to be created solely through situation and character: it is there in the setting.

The strength of Mrs Lessing's fiction comes from her comprehension both of the prevailing myths and of the forces which challenged them. She grew up in Southern Rhodesia and she shared in the culture she describes. The picture she gives us of the white-dominated society in the 1930s and 1940s is realistic and convincing. Her characters are seldom crude stereotypes (except when they seem almost to be parodying themselves), although they are shown to be quite capable of stereotyping other people. We as readers understand the characters' convictions and motivations to the extent that we too are shocked, although not unapproving, at the mode of their disillusionment. Doris Lessing's vision is ironic, but the narrator's distance is never so great as to keep the reader too far from the characters. The process is more subtle. Mrs Lessing seems to be saying 'yes, it was like this, and this' but her intelligence differentiates and takes her, and her readers, just that bit further than the limited perceptions of her characters. Or, she takes them to the limits of their perception, and then contrives a situation where they are made to realise their limitations. This is to say that in her early novels she is not a lofty, distant pundit. She is in there, as it were, amongst her characters, and perhaps this involvement is partly the result of the ambiguity suggested earlier: Africa is her home yet she is a white colonial, an alien. Her early upbringing was based on an acceptance of the colonial mythology. Her self-education developed through her increasing awareness of the mythopoeic processes, and her fiction charts her disentanglement from them.

The Grass is Singing (1950) is Mrs Lessing's first novel. She gave up her secretarial job to write it, and she took the manuscript to England with her in 1949. It was accepted by Michael Joseph, the first publisher to whom the manuscript was submitted, and from the first it proved very successful. It was reprinted several times, and translated into several languages.

The novel is set in Africa, and in the first chapter we learn that a white woman, Mary Turner, has been murdered by her black servant. We are then shown, in an extended flashback, her courtship and marriage. She had escaped from a childhood of misery and poverty to work happily in the town. In her thirties she marries a lonely farmer, Dick, who takes her to live on a remote farm in the bush. Mary is sexually cold and socially reserved, and her marriage is bitterly unhappy. The only intimate relationship she has in her life is with the black servant, Moses, who gains a subtle psychological dominance over her. When he sees the relationship threatened, he murders her.

In this first novel Doris Lessing rehearses themes which recur in her later work. These include the relationship between dominant and dominated races, the taboos which operate and the methods by which the *status quo* is maintained. We see the effect of the African landscape and climate on the whites, and the ways in which white aspirations are defeated. Mrs Lessing looks at female sexuality, and at the ways in which the balance of power is achieved between the sexes in her first close analysis of the dynamics of marriage. She also looks at the breakdown and fragmentation of an individual personality. *The Grass is Singing* is thus a convenient showcase, as it were, for the topics that are insisted upon, worked and reworked in her fiction: colonialism, politics, feminism, and a fascination with the unconscious as it is revealed in dreams and madness.

The colonial myth questioned in *The Grass is Singing* is that of white superiority and separateness from the native peoples. Thus the most shocking aspect of the novel becomes not so much the murder of Mary, but the neighbours' attitude to it. The Turners, through failure at farming, through poverty, and then through Mary getting herself murdered, seem somehow to have let the side down. The Turners' impoverished life-style and Mary's death have severely threatened white solidarity, a quality carefully cherished in the colonial society of the novel. The Turners are disliked from the start by their farming neighbours because they are so reclusive. The frontier traditions of hospitality are ignored, and Mary does not respond to friendly overtures from Charlie Slatter's wife, her nearest white neighbour. They do not even have a telephone, and they refuse to join in the local social activities. Mary even rejects the rare opportunities for 'women's talk' with the other farmers' wives, to Dick's initial surprise. 'They apparently did not recognise the need for *esprit de corps*: that, really, was why they were hated' (Ch. 1). Moreover, the Turners live in extremely primitive conditions, and this is a source of irritation to the scattered white community. 'Why, some natives (though not many thank heavens) had houses as good; and it would give them a bad impression to see white people living in such a way' (Ch. 1). This, of course, is a political and not an economic anxiety. If the natives perceive that they are, in whatever sense, as good as the whites, this perception may unleash all kinds of unthinkable aspirations. In the character of Tony Marston Doris Lessing illustrates a man in the process of becoming adjusted to the ways of white Rhodesia. Hired by Charlie

Slatter to take over the Turner's farm, he is still new enough to
the country to question the rules with which he is implicitly
expected to comply. Mrs Lessing uses him to express an
alternative view to the colonial myth. He is not a liberal in the
sense that he is committed to an ideology different from that of
the white colonialists; rather, he is still uncommitted to the
assumptions and mores of settler life. Tony is aware that the
motives for the murder are complicated by Mary's emotional
involvement with her black servant. 'He had his own ideas
about the murder, which could not be stated straight out, like
that, in black and white' (Ch. 1). The pun encapsulates the
colonials' fear of ambiguities. A kind of intellectual as well as
literal apartheid is practised in order to keep ideas clear and
separate. 'Grey areas' are forbidden because there is a direct
connection between the interbreeding of ideas and miscegenation.
Mary's murder has to be seen as unprovoked, since any
culpability on her part muddles the equation of black with guilt
and white with innocence. Charlie Slatter witnessed Mary's
relationship with Moses, and is appalled at her coy but terrified
acceptance of the servant's power. That Mary was sexually
attracted to Moses is almost unthinkable, and certainly
unspeakable. The white community 'behaved like a flock of
birds who communicate – or so it seems – by a kind of
telepathy' (Ch. 1). They knew, and simultaneously decided not
to know, hence the unnatural lack of gossip on Mary's death.

Tony too has to learn to hide his knowledge, to adopt the
double standards of his chosen country. We are told by the
narrator that 'When old settlers say, "One has to understand
the country," . . . They are saying, in effect, "Learn our ideas,
or otherwise get out' (Ch. 1). He soon realises that the murder
itself is relatively unimportant to the white community. Charlie
Slatter and the police sergeant are not concerned about Mary's
death; their 'instinctive horror and fear' (Ch. 1) is to do with the
threat to their entire social structure. Tony understands that
they are defending 'white civilisation', and that his view that 'it
takes two to make a murder . . . of this kind' is not wanted at
all. He is destroyed by his understanding. He abandons the
farm, and takes an office job. The people in the district pass
their own verdict on him: '"No guts", they said. "He should
have stuck it out"' (Ch. 1).

The impact of this novel derives largely from the

characterisation of Mary Turner. Her relationship with Moses is shown to be not out of character, but in fact a culmination of repressed feelings and incidents which are built up gradually throughout the text. When we first meet Mary she is in her mid-thirties, working in a town as a secretary, having escaped from an unhappy country childhood and a drunken father. Very early on the reader is made aware of her reluctance to assume adult sexuality. She still lives in a girls' hostel and dresses like a young girl. Her social life is full, but her men friends 'treated her just like a good pal, with none of this silly sex business' (Ch. 2). Mary overhears some friends talking about her marriage prospects. One of them says she is unlikely to marry: 'She just isn't like that, isn't like that at all' (Ch. 2). This denial of her sexual nature puzzles and upsets Mary, and she marries Dick to restore her self-esteem, but the marriage is a failure. The narrator depicts this failure in a way which prefigures the analyses of women's sexual identities in *The Children of Violence* sequence, and in *The Golden Notebook*. 'Women have an extraordinary ability to withdraw from the sexual relationship, to immunize themselves against it, in such a way that their men can be left feeling let down and insulted without having anything tangible to complain of. Mary did not have to learn this, because it was natural to her' (Ch. 3).

Mary despises her husband because he is a dreamer and a failure at farming. He begins schemes for tree planting, beekeeping, pigs and turkeys, but all these fall through. His ineptitude is further highlighted by the comparisons made between him and Charlie Slatter throughout the novel. The narrator makes the point early on that Charlie 'personified Society for the Turners' (Ch. 1) and we are made aware of the contrasts between them, epitomised by their farming methods. Charlie makes money because he exploits both the land and the native workforce; he was once fined thirty pounds for killing a workman. (Mrs Lessing leaves the reader to make the comparison between Charlie's fine and Moses's death penalty for the same offence.) He never fertilises his soil and he has cut down all the trees on his land. He grows profitable crops, but reinvests his money in mining concerns rather than in the farm. Dick, on the other hand, plants trees and looks after his land. He is reluctant to grow tobacco, however profitable, because he sees it as an 'inhuman' crop, requiring factory-like conditions with barns and grading sheds. He is intimately involved with his farm. We are told that 'he knew the veld he lived from as the natives knew it . . . off this farm he would wither and die' (Ch. 7). Yet Dick lacks the ruthless financial self-interest that he needs to farm successfully in Rhodesia, and Mary can see no future for them. She leaves him and returns to the town, but she sees she cannot simply resume her old life, and Dick collects her within a day. They resume their dismal marriage, with Mary mistaking the source of Dick's weakness. We are shown the relationship from Dick's point of view: 'she must learn that his feeling of defeat was not really caused by his failure as a farmer at all: his failure was her hostility towards him as a man' (Ch. 7). Later, we are presented with Mary's viewpoint:

> When she saw him weak and goal-less, and pitiful, she hated him, and the hate turned in on herself. She needed a man stronger than herself, and she was trying to create one out of Dick. If he had genuinely, simply, because of the greater strength of his purpose, taken the ascendancy over her, she would have loved him, and no longer hated herself for being tied to a failure'. (Ch. 8)

She becomes acutely depressed, and asks Dick if they can have a child. He has dreamt of having a family, but only when things are right between them, and so he refuses. For a short period Mary sees the farm and her marriage with absolute clear-sightedness. She sees Dick as a good man, but doomed to failure, and the vision is too painful to be borne without hope or escapism.

The new servant, Moses, enters Mary's life when she is in despair and therefore vulnerable. He bears a scar on his cheek because two years ago she had struck him with a whip for working too slowly in the fields. At that time she had had a momentary fear that he would attack her, and this fear remains. Nevertheless, there is an element of physical attraction in her attitude towards him. Early in the novel we are told that Mary thinks of Dick working alongside 'the reeking bodies of the working natives' (Ch. 5) and now we are told that 'The powerful, broad-built body fascinated her' (Ch. 8). Mary sees Moses half-naked, washing outside in the yard. He stops and waits for her to go away, and 'she was furious that perhaps he believed she was there on purpose; this thought, of course, was not conscious; it would be too much presumption, such unspeakable cheek for him to imagine such a thing' (Ch. 8). In that quotation the narrator has to speak for Mary the thoughts she has forbidden herself, in order for the reader to understand what is going on. Dick, tired of the endless sacking of servants, insists that Moses stay, and Mary feels wrenched between two opposing forces. When Moses himself gives notice she breaks down and begs him not to go. He treats her hysteria with calm authority, and thereafter there is a subtle change in their relationship. Again, the narrator expresses states of mind which Mary is unconscious of: 'her feeling was one of strong and irrational fear, a deep uneasiness, and even – though this she did not know, would have died rather than acknowledge – of some dark attraction' (Ch. 9).

Dreams are very important in Mrs Lessing's fiction. They are used to indicate the unconscious and often repressed thoughts and desires of the characters. Dreams also act as prophecy, or as rehearsals of actions as yet unconsidered by the conscious mind. Mary Turner dreams about Moses, frightening dreams where she is forced to touch him. She also dreams that Dick is dead, and she feels tremendous relief. This, however, turns to fear as Moses and her father approach, merged together in an image of menacing sexual dominance. In Jungian terms, Moses has come to represent for Mary her 'shadow' – the repressed and alien side of her personality that is in opposition to those aspects which she can acknowledge consciously. 'Black' and 'white' thus take on a symbolism which is of course latent throughout the novel, but which becomes increasingly more explicit towards the end. Moses represents the 'black', hidden side of Mary's nature, and she is terrified of his attraction for her, since this may force her to come into contact, not just with him, but with the dark forces of her own personality. Yet she does achieve this contact, and in the midst of her disintegration she realises that she has disproved the charge that she is sexually arid. One afternoon Tony Marston discovers Moses dressing Mary in her bedroom, his attitude one of 'indulgent uxoriousness' (Ch. 10). Tony tries to talk with her, but Mary seems cut off from his concern:

She said suddenly, 'They said I was not like that, not like

that, not like that.' It was like a gramophone that had got stuck at one point.

'Not like what?' he asked blankly.

'Not like *that*.' The phrase was furtive, sly, yet triumphant. (Ch. 10)

Mary's triumph is at the emergence of her sexuality, and it is important to her even though it is linked to the process of breakdown and madness.

Mary's breakdown is shown ambivalently. It is a theme which returns in Mrs Lessing's later fiction, where she frequently shows the process of 'breaking down', of madness, as a necessary stage to a greater awareness. Tony Marston glibly labels Mary's illness 'a complete nervous breakdown'. Then he questions this, deciding rather that 'she lives in a world of her own, where other people's standards don't count' (Ch. 10). This is not to say that Mary is consciously taking an ideological stand against apartheid: Mrs Lessing makes it clear that her need for Moses arises from a personal neurosis which has isolated her from ordinary marital and social contact. In the final chapter we are shown Mary's last day from her viewpoint. Her perspective is disturbed, but she is exhilarated by the beauty of the morning, and she is also clairvoyantly aware that she will be murdered at the end of the day. She walks off the paths into the bush for the first time since she has lived at the farm, and experiences its terrifying beauty and vitality. The bush symbolises, like Moses, the wild, uncultivated side of her nature, and she is frightened by it. She thinks that Tony might save her, but then remembers that she had hoped to be saved from herself long ago, when she married another young man from a farm. She has a vision of the house reclaimed by the bush after they have left it, and when Moses does finally attack her, that night, we are told 'And then the bush avenged itself: that was her last thought' (Ch. 11).

Doris Lessing does not attempt to convey the thoughts and feelings of Moses in this novel, and she has been criticised for this. He remains a cypher rather than a character whose personality and motivation we can understand. In an interview Doris Lessing says:

There was a long time when I thought that it was a pity I

ever wrote Moses like that, because he was less of a person
than a symbol. But it was the only way I *could* write him at
the time since I'd never *met* Africans excepting the servants
or politically, in a certain complicated way. But now I've
changed my mind again. I think it was the right way to write
Moses, because if I'd made him too individual it would've
unbalanced the book. I think I was right to make him a bit
unknown.[19]

Mrs Lessing's least successful short stories are where she
attempts to write from the point of view of black Africans, and
perhaps one has to accept the difficulty, if not the impossibility
of such a task without feeling guilty of an apartheid of the
imagination.

The Grass is Singing is an extraordinary first novel in its
assured treatment of its unusual subject matter. In the 1940s a
white woman's desire for a black servant was a theme as taboo
for a novelist in Rhodesia as it was for general conversation. In
writing about it, Doris Lessing questions the entire values of
Rhodesian white colonial society. She is not didactic, however;
there are no sermonising passages in the novel by an intrusive
narrator. She knows perfectly well that her plot and
characterisation are sufficiently powerful to convey her message.
This novel, rooted in colonialism, lays the foundation for much
of Doris Lessing's later work.

Doris Lessing has written numerous short stories about Africa
and in nearly all of them she describes a conflict between white
sensibility (or lack of it) and African culture. We are shown
both the European and the African experiences of exile and
alienation. The European exile causes the Africans' displacement,
forcing then to leave their tribal lands, and to live apart from
their families. Underlying her narratives is Mrs Lessing's
implacable message that Africa belongs to the Africans, so that
there is never a 'happy ending' for the settlers in the sense of
unconditional acceptance. Any coming to terms with their new
country is provisional or a compromise, or indeed, occasionally
an awareness of the impossibility of 'settling'. Even those
Europeans who feel themselves to be liberal and enlightened
are not exempt from Mrs Lessing's strictures. Some kinds of
liberalism, as shown in 'Little Tembi' or 'A Home for the

Highland Cattle' are seen to be as ineffectual as the most common attitudes of racial prejudice.

Some of the African stories are told from the point of view of a child or an adolescent, and through their openness to their surroundings we see the dawning realisation of strangeness, of differences, of unbridgeable gulfs. The child's perception is a useful device for the author because it enables her to show the registering of new awareness, a process not often made available to her adult characters who are too fixed in their views to see freshly. The stories about adult settlers concentrate more on their efforts to subdue the alien culture to their own. 'This was the Old Chief's Country' is one of Mrs Lessing's best known stories in which the action is seen predominantly through the eyes of a 14-year-old girl. Although the child has lived in Africa for many years, she has inherited an English tradition of landscape and literature, so that oak and ash trees are more familiar to her than the African shrubs all around her, and her fairy tales are Northern – of witches and woodcutters and snow. Walking in the bush she meets some natives and is struck by their dignity. She is introduced to the oldest of them, who is a tribal chief. She learns that the district she lives in once belonged to this chief and his ancestors, and this knowledge gives her a new perspective on Africa and her attitude to the natives: 'It seemed it was only necessary to let free that respect I felt when I was talking with old Chief Mshlanga, to let both black and white people meet gently, with tolerance for each other's differences: it seemed quite easy' (*Collected African Stories*, vol. 1, p. 17).

After discovering that their cook is the chief's son and heir, the girl decides to visit his home, out of curiosity. On the long walk to his village she travels through unfamiliar country and experiences terror of the bush for the first time. Here, Mrs Lessing suggests that the strangeness of Africa is unable to be alleviated because the folklore and culture which might make it accessible are not available to the white settler. Northern forests can be rendered harmless, made familiar, through stories of woodcutters and fairies. The African bush stays unknowable, a distance which is echoed by her reception at the village. On arriving she notices the difference between the village with its beautifully decorated, thatched huts, and the dirty, transient atmosphere of the native compound at the farm. She is welcomed distantly and formally by the chief, and can think of nothing to say to him. She returns home, feeling excluded: 'there was now a queer hostility in the landscape, a cold, hard, sullen indomitability that walked with me, as strong as a wall, as intangible as smoke: it seemed to say to me: you walk here as a destroyer' (*Collected African Stories*, vol. 1, p. 22).

The story ends with a row between her father and the old chief. A herd of goats has damaged one of her father's crops, and he keeps the goats in compensation. The native people were relying on the goats for food in the dry season, and their loss is serious. The chief says, in effect, that the white people have no right to his land, and both he and his son return to the bush. As an indirect result of this altercation the villagers are moved from their kraal to a distant native reserve. Thus, in miniature one might say, Doris Lessing illustrates the colonial takeover. Her protagonist, however, is more clear-sighted than the majority of colonials she writes about. The girl moves from total ignorance of the country and the people around her to the false impression that there is room for everyone, given a little mutual respect. Her final realisation is that no easy apologies will make her any less of a usurper, neither will Africa ever belong to her.

A similar story is revealed in 'A Sunrise on the Veld', which is told from the viewpoint of a boy of 15. He goes hunting on the veld in the early morning with his gun and his dogs. He feels strong and invincible: 'there is nothing I can't become, nothing I can't do; there is no country in the world I cannot make part of myself, if I choose' (*Collected African Stories*, vol. 1, p. 28). He hears a noise like a scream, and finds a dying buck being eaten by swarms of ants. He is appalled, but accepts this grim knowledge as part of the 'vast unalterable cruel veld'. Then he realises that the buck had had its leg broken by native hunters, which is why the ants attacked it. And he thinks of the times he has taken a shot at a buck, not always bothering to find out whether or not he has killed it. This shifts the responsibility from the impersonal forces of the veld to man's involvement with it, and he is left to contemplate the difference. During the narrative his mood changes from one of wild exhilaration in his own strength (dismissing the thought that he could ever break his ankle), to impersonal stoicism, to the gradual unwelcome awareness of his own potential to cause much suffering. It is a short and economically told story, but it resonates with meaning like an allegory. In a few minutes, the boy goes through stages of revelation that may not be universally learnt in generations. 'A Sunrise on the Veld' is a very good example of how Doris Lessing gives a local situation or incident a wider, even universal application, without explicitly analysing the point or commenting on the moral.

Many of Mrs Lessing's short stories show the ways in which the settlers are changed in their attempts to adapt to Africa. 'Leopard George' is such a story. From the beginning we see that George feels an affinity with Africa and its wildness. When choosing his land he rejects a beautiful, lush farm for five thousand acres of bush, and settles there. He builds himself a large house and a swimming pool, and employs native people whose leader formerly worked for George's father. Mrs Lessing describes the mutual respect between George and his 'bossboy', and adds, in parenthesis: 'This was in the early 'twenties, when a more gentle, almost feudal relationship was possible between good masters and their servants: there was space, then, for courtesy, bitterness had not yet crowded out affection' (*Collected African Stories*, vol. 1, pp. 170–1).

George is unmarried, and both his bossboy and his neighbours urge him to take a wife. He is considered slightly eccentric because he will not allow any animal to be killed or hunted on his farm, which 'was as good as a game reserve'. He appears to be satisfied with his solitary life, though we are not shown his interior thoughts. The narrator admits a diffidence in intruding on George's privacy:

> But it is not easy to ask of such a man, living in such a way, what it is he misses, if he misses anything at all. To ask would mean entering into what he feels during the long hours riding over the ridges of the kopje in the sunshine, with the grass waving about him like blond banners. It would mean understanding what made him one of mankind's outriders in the first place. (*Collected African Stories*, vol. 1, p. 173)

Thus Mrs Lessing suggests the sort of person George is, without analysing for us the psychological basis of his character, or his motivation. The narrator says of George: 'Perhaps he really did feel he ought to marry.' The 'perhaps' refuses the authorial

privilege of absolute knowledge, and the unknowability of a
character is more realistic than if we wholly understood all
George's innermost thoughts and impulses.

At weekends George holds bathing parties, where the young
girls of the neighbourhood flirt with him. At one of these parties
a native African girl appears, wanting to talk to him. She gives
the clear impression of being his mistress; his white guests
notice this and feel 'an irritation which was a reproach for not
preserving appearances' (p. 178). George is very angry with the
girl. She is the daughter or grand-daughter (again, the narrator
is uncertain) of his bossboy, Smoke, and her liaison with George
has lasted for five years. He sends for Smoke and complains
that the girl is making trouble. George arranges for her to be
sent to a mission school to get her out of his way. A few weeks
later another, younger girl presents herself to George. He tries
to make the arrangement perfectly clear. He pays her and
insists that she return home after their love-making, even
though she is terrified of the bush at night. The next day Smoke
is very upset, and George realises with horror that the young
girl is his new wife. When she comes to him again, he sends her
straight home. She is too frightened of the bush to go on her
own, and George cannot understand this. He is not frightened
of the bush, and he feels obscurely that the girl should not be
afraid of her natural habitat. In the morning Smoke comes to
tell George that the girl has not arrived home. For the first time
George feels fear growing inside him, a fear of the African
landscape. He takes his gun and kills a leopard. In the morning
he finds its cave, where there are fresh human bones amongst
the other debris.

Killing the leopard in revenge is not enough, however: 'He
did not know what satisfaction it was he needed' (p. 191).
Neither are we told. The narrator says only that 'there was a
hurt place in him, and a hungry anger that no work could
assuage' (p. 191). After this episode George fills his stables with
horses and dogs, and establishes regular leopard hunts. He kills
a wounded leopard with the butt of his rifle, and eventually his
body becomes covered in scars from his wounds. He marries a
woman with grown-up children, and the story ends abruptly.

Significantly it is the omissions in this narrative that are the
most potent carriers of meaning. We are not told specifically
why George does not marry a suitable young white girl early

on, or why he gets impatient with his house parties and rides off alone into the bush. But it is implied that he feels more akin to Africa and the African than to his white compatriates. Thus he oversteps the unspoken boundaries of the white/black division. Mere prostitution of the native girl would have been acceptable, it is suggested, a business-like arrangement understood by everyone. But George muddles it by affection. He sometimes allows the girl to spend the night with him, and buys her presents in addition to paying her cash. She in turn breaks the rules by allowing herself to be seen by his white visitors at a weekend party. The second girl expresses her fear of the bush, and George is impatient because she feels fear and he does not. But of course her fear is based on an intimate and realistic knowledge of its dangers. Again, we are not told why her death completely changes George's life. Her disappearance engenders in George a new and stark recognition of the African bush, which mocks his former affinity with it. He feels guilt for sleeping with Smoke's wife, and he feels guilt when the girl is killed by the leopard, but he displaces his anger from himself to the animals. His earlier feelings about Africa are destroyed: 'For him, now, the landscape was simply a home for leopards' (p. 191). For all his sense of belonging, for all his love of its wildness, and his irritation with white 'civilisation', George is finally frustrated by the Africa he thought he knew. It seems almost that he is punished for his arrogance in having assumed such knowledge. He cannot, ultimately, transcend his foreignness; he cannot become part of Africa because his skin is white and his ways are essentially European.

In her African writings Doris Lessing works both within and beyond the colonial experience. She understands the rigorous limitations of colonial society which is formed and kept cohesive by maintaining its own narrow boundaries. But she has also achieved the feat of imaginatively stepping outside its borders – and this does not automatically follow her literally having done so by leaving Africa for England. This extended vision enables her to see beyond the false colonial myths of white superiority and the necessity of blacks and whites remaining separate. Hence her African short stories arise from a kind of irony engendered by perceiving the gap between the myths and the African reality. The price of 'settling' is an acceptance of the myths, of making a home amongst them. But Doris Lessing's

home has long since been reclaimed by the bush, and
appropriately, for she has always been engaged in the process of
making herself homeless, of leaving, of moving on.

3

The Children of Violence

The *Children of Violence* sequence was published between 1952 and 1969 and consists of five novels: *Martha Quest* (1952); *A Proper Marriage* (1954); *A Ripple from the Storm* (1958); *Landlocked* (1965) and *The Four-Gated City* (1969). In this chapter these five novels will be looked at in turn, but it is important to remember that their publication was interspersed with that of other novels, novellas and short stories. This accounts, in part, for the great differences between the early and later books in the series. Mrs Lessing has called the *Children of Violence* a *Bildungsroman*, that is, the story of a young person's development and education in society. The story is not, however, written from a single consistent viewpoint, as if Mrs Lessing had reached a certain stage of understanding and written all five novels from that particular perspective. Over the seventeen years between the publication of *Martha Quest* and *The Four-Gated City* she examines a wide range of social, personal and artistic assumptions, including the problems inherent in writing fiction. Thus, when she returns to the sequence after a gap of seven years with *Landlocked* in 1965 (having published *The Golden Notebook* in 1962), there is a noticeable change in her angle of vision. What we have in the *Children of Violence* is the effect of the author's evolving consciousness of her style and her fictive priorities. There is a change of emphasis which is not just to do with the heroine's development, but with the author's also.

This brings us to the question of autobiography and fiction. There is no doubt from the evidence of Mrs Lessing's interviews and non-fictional works that the *Children of Violence* is highly autobiographical, and that the character of Martha Quest owes a great deal to the character of her author. Fact and fiction blur together: it is quite often difficult to disentangle them, and confusing to attempt to do so. Mrs Lessing has said?:

35

I get impatient with this thing about 'autobiographical'. You can't write about anything you haven't experienced or imagined – it has to be your experience, your imagination. The point is that the very moment you start writing about something that has happened, it's no longer yours – all the other things come in and change it; you remember something like it, or somebody who looked like that. It's impossible to write autobiographically . . . it's impossible to have an experience that other people haven't had, or aren't having.[20]

In other words she refuses to claim any experience or insight as unique, as if the description of her work as 'autobiographical' were a criticism of narrowness or elitism. It is not necessary for the reader to consider the events in Mrs Lessing's life in relation to those in her fiction, as long as the fiction remains convincing on its own terms. It is important only when an author fails to subsume the raw material of real life into fiction; that is, when the reasons for a novel's failure are at issue. With Doris Lessing, as with any other author, one can welcome whatever extra dimension a knowledge of her early life brings to a reading of the novels. *Children of Violence* is, for the most part, coherent as a work of art in its own right. If a reader is familiar with Mrs Lessing's non-fiction then the novels will resonate with echoes of her real life; but they will also do so if nothing is known about the author at all.

The plot of *Children of Violence* covers a time-span from the 1930s to the year 2000. It tells the story of Martha Quest, a white colonial living in a country called Zambesia, whose parents have led unsuccessful lives farming in the bush. She leaves home in her teens and goes to the town, where she marries a civil servant and has a child. Her marriage is unsatisfactory, and she leaves her husband and daughter. She joins a Marxist group which includes European refugees and British airmen who are training in Africa during the Second World War. Martha, having divorced her husband, remarries, this time to a German Jew who is a committed Marxist. She spends much of her time attending political meetings and working for the group, but she is not happy and her dreams reflect her dissatisfaction. Her marriage again deteriorates, and she has a deep and passionate involvement with a Polish Jew, a settler called Thomas Stern. Through this relationship she begins to understand herself. She leaves her husband and goes to England after the war. In London she works for a man called Mark Coldridge, whose wife is considered unbalanced. Martha takes over the running of the house and helps to look after the children of the family. She becomes involved with radical political and social issues, and she also forms a close association with Mark's wife Lynda. Through their mutual interest in mysticism Martha begins to see a way of living without necessarily aligning herself to movements or causes. She begins to recognise and then to practise new skills such as telepathy which she realises are within the potential of the human race, and which may be essential skills for survival after a nuclear holocaust. The novel series ends with documents written after such a holocaust, describing a new generation of children with extra-sensory perception and other qualities necessary for their development in their new world.

Doris Lessing has called *Children of Violence* 'a study of the individual conscience in its relations with the collective'.[21] Neither the 'individual conscience' nor the 'collective' remain consistent throughout the novels. Martha's surname 'Quest' obviously suggests a search, a journeying towards some kind of goal, or grail, and we see her clash time and again with outside forces and groups. The 'collective' is variously the white Zambesian society of her parents' generation, the young colonial society of her own generation, a Marxist group, and post-war London intelligentsia. She is both dependent upon, and reacts against, all these factions, constantly redefining herself through her relations with them. The earlier novels in this sequence concentrate primarily on Martha's adolescence, marriage and motherhood. When her discontent with traditional female roles forces her to leave her husband and child we see her in what should be a wider context, that of politics, though this in turn becomes an illusory vision of freedom. In the later novels she transcends the 'individual versus the collective' dichotomy, first through erotic experience and then through mysticism. Her perspective widens, and similarly the reader's understanding of Martha and her milieu is expanded. In *Martha Quest* and *A Proper Marriage* she fills the whole canvas, so to speak. In *A Ripple from the Storm* and *Landlocked* other issues are jostling for space. Finally, in *The Four-Gated City*, we see her almost from a cosmic perspective. As Martha becomes aware of her relative

insignificance in the universe, the reader too sees her as a
minute part of a much larger picture. In cinematic terms, the
close-up gives way to a medium and then a long shot, and this
reflects Martha's states of mind and being: in the early novels
she is obsessed with herself and what she thinks, and how an
individual should behave in relation to the needs of mankind.
In *The Four-Gated City* in particular, she is much more interested
in methods of transcending the individual consciousness than in
merging it with a specific political or social group. She is
concerned about the evolution of the kind of knowledge needed
for survival in the twentieth century and beyond, and in this
her 'self' becomes irrelevant; her vision extends far wider.

Martha Quest begins with the 15-year-old Martha restless and
bored on her parents' isolated farm. Nicole Ward Jouve[22] has
pointed out the significant omission of any description of
Martha's childhood. At 15 she is formed, and it is this
character – accentuated, modified, battered, reshaped, but
essentially the same – with whom the reader is involved
throughout the five volumes of the series. But we are not
allowed to see what influences created and formed the
foundations of this individual except in tiny retrospective
glimpses or what we can deduce from Martha's relationship
with her parents. So here, very early on, arises the problem of
relating fiction and autobiography. Has Doris Lessing avoided
giving us Martha's childhood because it is also her childhood,
at once too clear, too distant and too painful to fictionalise? It is
not until *The Memoirs of a Survivor* (1975) that she tackles this
difficult area. Here the omission means that we have to take
Martha's character on trust, as a given state, and it is a
peculiar gap given the centrality of Martha to the whole work.

Martha longs to get away from her parents, and she pursues
two courses to this end – intellectual and emotional. She reads
books borrowed from two clever Jewish brothers, on sexuality,
sociology and economics. This kind of reading confirms her
idea of herself as exceptional, as different from her parents. She
is also aware of the ritual transitions to womanhood as a
possible way to a new life. Invited to her first dance by some
neighbours, she makes herself a beautiful white evening gown,
having rejected a childish pink dress suggested by her

mother. She hopes for, but does not receive, her parents' acknowledgement that she has grown up.

For at that moment when she had stood before them, it was in a role which went far beyond her, Martha Quest: it was timeless . . . it should have been a moment of abnegation, when she must be kissed, approved, and set free. Nothing of this kind could Martha have put into words, or even allowed herself to feel; but now, in order to regain that freedom where she was not so much herself as a creature buoyed on something that flooded into her as a knowledge that she was moving inescapably through an ancient role, she must leave her parents who destroyed her. (Pt. 1, Ch. 3)

But Martha's inability truly to develop beyond the influence of her mother is a thread running through the novels, and an unconscious motivation for much of her unconventional behaviour.

Early in *Martha Quest* we are given two passages that seem inconsistent in tone with the rest of the novel. In the first one we are shown Martha day-dreaming, and the substance and symbolism of her dream informs the whole of *Children of Violence*:

She looked away over the ploughed land, across the veld to the Dumfries Hills, and refashioned that unused country to the scale of her imagination. There arose, glimmering whitely over the harsh scrub and the stunted trees, a noble city, set foursquare and colonnaded along its falling flower-bordered terraces. There were splashing fountains, and the sound of flutes; and its citizens moved, grave and beautiful, black and white and brown together; and these groups of elders paused, and smiled with pleasure at the sight of the children – the blue-eyed, fair-skinned children of the North playing hand in hand with the bronze-skinned, dark-eyed children of the South. Yes, they smiled and approved these many-fathered children, running and playing among the flowers and the terraces, through the white pillars and tall trees of this fabulous and ancient city. (Pt. 1, Ch. 1)

This is a vision of the imagination, but Martha also has a mystical experience, a kind of ecstasy in which she feels at one with the earth: 'during that space of time (which was timeless) she understood quite finally her smallness, the unimportance of humanity . . . she knew futility; that is, what was futile was her own idea of herself and her place in the chaos of matter. What was demanded of her was that she should accept something quite different' (Pt. 1, Ch. 2). These two passages, the vision and the mystical experience, are lyrical in style, and if they seem inconsistent with the more prosaic tone of *Martha Quest*, they are nevertheless pointers to Martha's potential as a visionary, and also to the author's intention of developing these themes later on. It is not until *The Four-Gated City* that they are explored much more fully, and it is not until she is much older that Martha fully apprehends the meaning of her mystical experience.

In describing Martha's relationships with men Doris Lessing shows how her aspirations towards energetic independence are blocked by her feminine passivity. She is claimed by different men, and her compliance is at odds with the passionate, impatient temperament we have seen her display against her parents. 'Martha learned that she was Donovan's girl' (Pt. 1, Ch. 2); 'she understood that she was now Perry's girl and not Donovan's' (Pt. 1, Ch. 2). Even her decision to marry is couched in passive terms: 'By the end of the evening, it was decided that they would marry' (Pt. 1, Ch. 3). In an attempt to assert her independence from the Sports Club crowd, Martha loses her virginity to a Jewish musician, who is not accepted by them, but even then her impulse is one of pity and defiance, rather than what she really wants. Throughout this novel Martha submits to new experiences, not so much for what they can offer, but to show her more clearly what she is. She seeks to define herself, but she goes about it by accepting new situations, new people, in the hope that they will define her. Such definition is needed, because we see that Martha's personality is highly fragmented, and that she is aware of this: 'it was as if half a dozen entirely different people inhabited her body, and they violently disliked each other, bound together by only one thing, a strong impulse of longing' (Pt. 1, Ch. 2). Martha sees escape from the farm to the town, then sex, then marriage, then political activity, as potentials for fulfilment. We are shown that each experience in turn fails to satisfy her, and the longing to

integrate the disparate elements of her character remains until
she is able to acknowledge and accept the worst of them.

The contradictory emotions Martha feels about marriage,
and yet the inexorable rush towards it are astutely conveyed.
Given Martha's views about the Sports Club men it is surprising
that she marries one of them. But Douglas reads the *New
Statesman* and this allows her to invest him with qualities he
does not, nor ever can, possess. Martha is not oblivious of
Douglas' unsuitability: 'she was, in fact, already feeling a
creeping disgust of him. It would, however, all be all right
when they were married' (Pt. 4, Ch. 3). Douglas colludes with
this, and although worried by her coolness towards him 'he
used the ancient formula, she'll be all right once we're married'
(Pt. 4, Ch. 3). These clichés enable the reader to understand
more than the characters, and the narrator makes sure that we
realise the incompatibility of the couple. How can sharp, clever
Martha Quest be so stupid? At the same time, her action, or
rather her inaction, has a ring of horrible accuracy, and it is
not difficult to understand her deluded acquiescence to the
marriage.

Douglas and Martha make a ritual visit to the farm to
introduce Douglas to Mr and Mrs Quest, and Martha is
perversely disappointed at her parents' lack of opposition to the
marriage. 'Surely there should have been some real moment of
crisis, a point of choice?' (Pt. 4, Ch. 3) Martha wants to be
forced to make a positive choice, she wants clear endings and
beginnings. Instead, she settles for acquiescence to events, in
the hope that she will be changed by them. Just as Adolph
King, as a person, was almost irrelevant to Martha's sexual
initiation, since the initiation itself was what mattered, so
Douglas Knowell seems irrelevant to her marriage. The state of
marriage is an end in itself. Martha's choice of marriage is her
escape route from the life she has been leading in the town, just
as the town life was an escape from the farm. Ironically, in
fleeing from her parents and their values, she ends up in a
marriage as claustrophobic as theirs.

The seeds of Martha's political consciousness are sown in
Martha Quest, but politics do not occupy much of the novel. Joss
Cohen introduces her to the Left Book Club, and on reading a
left-wing periodical for the first time she immediately feels at

home: 'for here were ideas which she had been defending guiltily for years used as the merest commonplaces' (Pt. 2, Ch. 3). There is a moment of choice between Douglas and the Cohen brothers who are speaking at an open-air meeting, and Martha chooses Douglas. But already, even before she is married, the idea of leaving Douglas is in her mind, and the reader is aware that political action is one of the avenues she might follow.

In *Martha Quest* Doris Lessing shows Martha's relationship with the African landscape. When she is longing to leave the farm she loses her childhood love of the bush, and the wide countryside and blue skies become, paradoxically, claustrophobic to her. But after her affair with Adolph, Martha finds herself thinking about the seasons on the farm, and we are given a lyrical and nostalgic description of the fresh growth produced by the rains. When Douglas and Martha visit her parents, she is newly astonished by the veld, and the narrator gives a heartfelt glimpse of what it means to be an exile:

> This naked embrace of earth and sky, the sun hard and strong overhead, pulling up the moisture from foilage, from soil, so that the swimming glisten of heat is like a caress made visible, this openness of air, everything visible for leagues, so that the circling hawk (the sun glancing off its wings) seems equipoised between sun and boulder – this frank embrace between the lifting breast of the land and the deep blue warmth of the sky is what exiles from Africa dream of; it is what they sicken for, no matter how hard they try to shut their minds against the memory of it. (Pt. 4, Ch. 3)

This long sentence, phrase upon phrase of description, gives the impression of an ever-accelerating memory, gathering momentum as the images return. The personification of the land and the tone of the language, reminiscent of D. H. Lawrence, involve the reader in the physicality of the African heat, and the sense of well-being is heightened by the use of the contrasting verb 'sicken'; it covers both a sense of physical illness and emotional apathy, as if both were entailed in being exiled from the warmth of Africa. This passage is very moving, and the intensification of the narratorial language reveals how much Mrs Lessing remembers and misses the land of her upbringing.

In *Martha Quest*, many specific themes are introduced: feminism, marriage, politics, the vision of an ideal society – all these are set up, heavy with possibilities. But in this novel we are also given the counter-balance of their negation, of non-progression, of a frustrating repetition. Martha's longings are for growth, for wholeness, but we see already the ways in which she almost wilfully prevents her own integration. The marriage which ends the novel is a kind of mockery of conventional happy endings. Martha is appallingly distressed, signs documents she has not read, and snaps at her mother during the ceremony. We are given an ironic vignette of Mrs Quest shaking the hand of the magistrate afterwards, and saying 'Mr. Maynard, you must agree with me, it's *such* a relief when you get your daughter properly married!' (Pt. 4, Ch. 3). The next novel in the sequence is entitled *A Proper Marriage* and the word 'proper' is (by this time, unsurprisingly) thoroughly undermined in the course of it.

Near the beginning of *A Proper Marriage* Martha quarrels with Douglas, and then acquiesces to his love-making, through 'an instinct to please'. We are given her thoughts: 'love was the key to every good; love lay like a mirage through the gates of sex. If this was not true, then nothing was true, and the beliefs of a whole generation were illusory' (Pt. 1, Ch. 1). The *Children of Violence* sequence of novels charts Martha's disillusion with sex and with falling in love. Although in *Landlocked* she has a beneficial relationship involving both, they seem in Mrs Lessing's canon phases to be grown through, early stages of development which must be left behind if real psychical progress is to be made.

In *A Proper Marriage* Martha is shown to be fighting against the boredom of a conventional housewife. Her newly won privacy from her parents is lost again to her husband. She is exasperated when she discovers that she is pregnant, particularly when she realises that people are suggesting that she and Douglas 'had' to get married 'for she felt this was an insult towards them as being free beings able to do as they wished' (Pt. 1, Ch. 3). In order to defy their husbands' proprietary fussiness about their health, Martha and a pregnant friend, Alice, succumb to an impulse to go out into the driving rain of the wet season. In one of the most powerful scenes in the *Children of Violence* series, Martha and Alice tear off their clothes and plunge with abandon into the waist-high grass and mud:

[Martha] ran on blindly, her hair a sodden mat over her eyes, her arms held out in front to keep the whipping grass off her face. She almost ran into a gulf that opened under her feet. It was a pot-hole, gaping like a mouth, its red crumbling sides swimming with red water. Above it the long heavy grass almost met. Martha hesitated, then jumped straight in. A moment of repugnance, then she loosened deliciously in the warm rocking of the water. She stood to her knees in heavy mud, the red thick water closed below her shoulders. (Pt. 2, Ch. 2)

The exaltation of this experience doesn't last. As soon as she gets home Martha baths: 'She now hated to think of the mud of the vlei in her pores' (Pt. 2, Ch. 2). Nevertheless, the episode stands out as an instinctive healing impulse (again, there are Lawrentian echoes) which allows Martha temporary freedom through an irrational but naturally spontaneous action. Later, in *The Four-Gated City*, Mrs Lessing returns to the irrational as a source of healing and of knowledge.

Martha's pregnancy claims more and more of her attention, and the narrative is taken over by the pregnancy and childbirth, just as Martha is. During the birth of her baby Martha is astonished and angry at her inability to control her body or her mind. Gripped with pain, she is totally unable to imagine a painless state; released from pain a few seconds later she can no longer imagine or even remember the pain: 'It was a complete failure of her, the free spirit' (Pt. 2, Ch. 3). The words 'free' and 'freedom' gather irony in Doris Lessing's novels, and Martha's vision of herself as 'free' is usually juxtaposed with her extreme passivity, her definition of herself by events and people around her.

Her new role is that of a mother, and when Douglas is called up to fight in the Second World War, she is left to manage alone. She engages in a domestic battle of wills with her baby daughter Caroline, who refuses to eat without coercion, and Martha endures the boredom of being in a small flat with a baby, day after day. She sees their troubled relationship as inevitable: 'you and I are just victims, my poor child, you can't help it, I can't help it, my mother couldn't help it, and her mother . . .' (Pt. 3, Ch. 2). Mrs Quest interferes triumphantly with the baby's upbringing, causing Martha almost unbearable tension. Her belief that parents invariably cause their children irreparable harm stems from her appalling relationship with her own mother, and it enables her to leave Caroline when she separates from Douglas. Martha believes that she is setting Caroline free from the vicious legacy of parental tyranny. But somehow Martha's conviction of this does not ring true, even though the narrator withholds any ironic judgement on her at this point. Martha's boredom with the child, yet her tenderness for her, sound authentic. Her farewell – 'You'll be perfectly free, Caroline. I'm setting you free' (Pt. 4, Ch. 4) – sounds false, as if Martha means 'I'm setting myself free'. There is no help from the narrator to support this interpretation, only an uneasy ambiguity which suggests that here is another point in the novels where autobiography and fiction are in unresolved tension. (Doris Lessing also left her children when she left her first husband, and it may be difficult to write about this even in the distancing guise of fiction.) Martha's rationale lacks conviction and seems unnecessary even. The truth of the situation is that she will die emotionally and spiritually if she stays with Douglas. So she leaves, not really for the airman with whom she is temporarily in love, but for the heady politics of Marxism.

Martha's education in this novel is continued by Solly Cohen. Shortly after her marriage she had visited him where he was living in a commune in the Coloured quarter of the town. Impulsively she asked to live there too, as if her marriage did not exist. When her life with Douglas becomes unbearable, she contacts her left-wing acquaintances, who invite her to a meeting to raise money for 'Our Allies', which now include Russia. She buys some literature at the meeting, and for the first time in her life (she is now 22) reads about the Russian revolution. The reader is reminded of her introduction to the *New Statesman* some years earlier: 'It was as if her eyes had been opened and her ears made to hear; it was like a rebirth. For the first time in her life she had been offered an ideal to live for' (Pt. 2, Ch. 2). The biblical rhetoric is of course intentional, and expresses the force of her instant conversion, and her sense of moving swiftly from the stifling enclosure of marriage and motherhood to the thrilling horizons of a political movement. Thus *A Proper Marriage* ends in a similar vein to *Martha Quest*: Martha escapes from one circle of tedium and begins a wider, new life. But the reader should be alerted by this time to the irony of her 'escape'; by now it is clear that Martha is fleeing from the contradictions in her own nature, and it is only a self-confrontation that can free her. Meanwhile, however, the Communist Party offers her a means of defining herself anew.

Between the publication of *A Proper Marriage* in 1954 and its sequel *A Ripple from the Storm* in 1958, Doris Lessing published a separate novel, called *Retreat to Innocence*, in 1956. It is typical of Mrs Lessing's method of working that she often uses short stories, or plays, or even other novels and non-fiction to rehearse themes that reappear later in what might be called the mainstream of her work. By combining both a personal relationship and political propaganda, *Retreat to Innocence* provides a bridge between the emphasis on Martha's marriage and her later political commitment. It also enables Mrs Lessing to write out some of her feelings about the insularity of the English, a theme reiterated in her non-fiction work *In Pursuit of the English* (1960). *Retreat to Innocence* is about frustration: frustration with middle-class self-satisfaction, with the refusal of the young to be politically involved, and with the resolute anti-intellectualism of the society she describes.

The heroine, a young girl called Julia Barr, is the daughter of a wealthy but liberal-minded baronet who lives in Norfolk. She works in London, and her life is a reaction against her free-thinking parents. She keeps her flat tidy, and her bedroom is neat and frilled. She has a conventional boy-friend called Roger who is a civil servant, and she is a virgin. Julia meets a Jewish Czech refugee called Jan Brod, a communist who is much older than she is. In attempts to understand him, Julia sleeps with him, and types the manuscript of a book he has written about the Second World War. She tries to pull strings to get him British citizenship, and through her father's influence attempts to get him a better job. These efforts rebound, and Jan is forced to return to Eastern Europe. Julia finally marries her dull civil servant.

In this novel Mrs Lessing's approach to her theme is dialectical. She sets up potent oppositions: Jan's age versus Julia's youth; intellectual power versus naïve simplicity; European experience versus English innocence; communist versus capitalist; radical versus bourgeois. The problem for the reader is that the relationship between Jan and Julia is very unconvincing, because they represent Doris Lessing's thesis and antithesis, rather than becoming lively characters with a dynamic of their own. They are both stereotyped (although ideologically Doris Lessing understands Jan Brod better than she does Julia Barr) and so far apart that their meeting and attraction seems forced on the reader as a device rather than as the result of their motivations or inclinations. In fact, Julia does begin to change in response to Jan, but she is disturbed by the fragmenting effect he has on her identity. She wonders who she would be if she found herself a room in a part of London unknown to her. Interestingly, this prefigures Kate Brown's quest in *The Summer Before the Dark*. The difference is that Kate does find herself a room in a strange part of London, and does discover who she is. Julia rejects the route to this discovery, and returns to the safety of Roger.

A theme which interests Mrs Lessing and which recurs in her fiction is the generation gap, and the difficulties of bridging it. Julia is jealous of her parents' generation, and what she sees as their awful strength. In turn Julia's father tells her that he understands the difficulties for her of being handed everything on a plate. Implicit in Doris Lessing's recurring irritation with the generation succeeding hers is its refusal to carry on the struggle, its refusal to take up the baton handed on from its battle-worn elders. In her later novels Mrs Lessing is very scathing about the ineffectiveness of the young to cause change; in this novel we see the first signs of her frustration.

Retreat to Innocence contains a long eulogy to Stalin, in which Jan Brod compares him with the Messiah. Doris Lessing published this novel before the Twentieth Party Congress, and her attitude to communism is less equivocal here than in *A Ripple from the Storm*. It is her only piece of work that can be called propagandist, and the lack of its own inner life is consequently not surprising. Ironically, despite its political content, it is one of Doris Lessing's few attempts at an 'English' realist novel. The irony is that *Retreat to Innocence* is a novel that

could only have been written by someone who is neither English
nor European, but who is looking on at the two types with the
detachment that comes from belonging to neither category. It is
a novel full of short stories and scattered anecdotes, including a
wonderful joke when a policeman is looking at the untidy,
'artistic' room of the Czech-born Jan Brod, littered with books
and wine-glasses, and asks him dubiously if he is a Bohemian.
Nevertheless, there is no linking organic growth inside the
novel; the theme is imposed from the outside. Its discontent is
not yet with communism but with England, and the apparent
carelessness of a younger generation. In her next novel, *A
Ripple from the Storm*, she takes up the theme of Marxism in
wartime Rhodesia, which she calls Zambesia. But by the time
she writes that novel the Twentieth Party Congress and the
Hungarian revolution have taken place, Mrs Lessing has left the
Communist Party, and her perspective has changed.

In an interview with Florence Howe, Doris Lessing talks about
the political group she joined in Southern Rhodesia: 'There was
a time in my life when I was a member of a Communist group
which was pure – they had no contact with any kind of reality.
It must have been blessed by Lenin from his grave, it was so
pure.'[23] *A Ripple from the Storm* draws on this experience, and in
this novel Mrs Lessing details Martha's commitment to a
political cause. Her youthful vision of the ideal city is rekindled,
only this time she sees a way of making it come true through
the application of Marxist theory. When she and Jasmine, a
political colleague and friend, see a little ragged black child,
they know that 'because of their vision, he was protected and
saved: the future they dreamed of seemed just around the
corner; they could almost touch it. Each saw an ideal town,
clean, noble and beautiful, soaring up over the actual town they
saw' (Pt. 1, Ch. 1). But while Martha seeks to make real her
ideals, the Communist Party becomes more and more remote
from reality; while she seeks her own wholeness in the ideological
union of belief and action, the group gradually falls apart
because it cannot itself achieve this integration.

A Ripple from the Storm is probably the least interesting of the
Children of Violence novels, partly because it is very difficult to
convey and sustain a stultifying sense of boredom without *being*
boring. The agendas, the procedures, the rhetoric of the party

meetings are tedious, even to some of the participants, and even though Mrs Lessing's overall tone is ironic, this is not sufficiently enlivening to maintain the reader's interest. What is shown and is of more interest is Martha's initial naïvety and her growing awareness that the group is never going to be in touch with the working class (i.e. the Africans) for whose benefit it is intended. At an early meeting, Anton Hesse, a German Jewish refugee, gives the group an outline of Marxist history. It begins 'Comrades, this is the dawn of human history' and Martha becomes enthralled as she listens to it. Some of the group, however, are working-class airmen and do not understand what he's saying because he uses such long words. One of the group, Tommy, acts as an unconsciously ironic foil to reflect the impracticality of the Marxist ideals. He tries hard to understand what is going on, but he is very conscious of his lack of education. Jasmine therefore lends him *War and Peace* so that he can learn about the background to the Russian revolution.

The group is sustained for a while on a collective fantasy about its future effectiveness. They draw up a 150-page document on how the colony should be run under communism, voting on it clause by clause. It makes racial prejudice illegal, and it plans for all contingencies, including economic boycotts and war. Maisie, one of the girls in the group, puts forward a commonsense criticism pointing out that there is no chance of actually implementing the plan, since the communists are not even standing for election. This is considered irrelevant, but eventually the group disintegrates because most of them come to realise that its function is purely theoretical. Martha says 'we talk and talk and analyse and make formulations, but what are we doing? What are we changing?' (Pt. 2, Ch. 1). Ironically, the only black African member is a spy planted by the local magistrate, who has no real cause to worry about the revolutionary capacity of this tiny, self-divided party. When the group is disbanded, however, 'Martha felt herself cut off from everything that had fed her imagination: until this moment she had been part of the grandeur of the struggle in Europe, part of the Red Army, the guerillas in China, the French underground, and the partisans in Italy, Yugoslavia and Greece' (Pt. 4, Ch. 4). But, in Zambesia, her fervour has been poured into a cause which does not enable her to get closer to the Utopia of her dreams.

Martha's embrace of the Communist Party includes her marriage with the group leader, Anton Hesse. She has had a brief affair with an airman after leaving her husband, and when he has gone, she feels incomplete. Mrs Lessing gives us a description not only of Martha, but of the kind of woman who depends on a relationship with a man to give her an identity:

> If the man goes away there is left an empty space filled with shadows. She mourns for the temporarily extinct person she can only be with a man she loves; she mourns him who brought her 'self' to life. She lives with the empty space at her side, peopled with the images of her own potentialities until the next man walks into the space, absorbs the shadows into himself, creating her, allowing her to be her 'self' – but a new self, since it is his conception which forms her. (Pt. 1, Ch. 3)

This is a very important passage, because this kind of woman recurs in Mrs Lessing's fiction, and is often shown to be aware of maintaining an illusion that for her to be without a man is to be free. Martha's relationship with Anton again is determined by her passivity. When she is ill, he visits her in bed and kisses her, and: 'She was aware that he had again kissed her on the forehead and hot nausea came with the thought: well, that means now Anton and I will be together' (Pt. 2, Ch. 1). Anton is threatened with internment in a camp for enemy aliens if he continues his affair with Martha, and she marries him to allow him the freedom to continue his work for the Communist Party. There is no reason why she should not have broken off the affair instead, but Martha cannot yet be herself without a man, and she marries Anton, meanwhile assuring herself that 'it's nothing but a formality after all' (Pt. 3, Ch. 2).

Their married life is not happy. Anton is not a good sexual partner and, irritatingly, talks constantly to Martha about his dead wife, Grete. Martha protects herself 'by resting in imagination on the man who would enter her life and make her what she knew she could be' (Pt. 4, Ch. 1). Anton has no sense of humour, and when Martha makes a joke about Stalin he refuses to speak to her for a month. She realises that for the marriage to work, she has to act the role of a charming little girl, to whom Anton can be kind and patronising. Not surprisingly, she comes to feel that the marriage is hopeless, and determines that they will separate after the war is over. *A Ripple from the Storm* ends on a low note. The communist group has disbanded, and Martha is static, locked in a futile and deadening marriage. There is a sense of sterility, of wasted energy and dull exhaustion, not only thematically, but also in the tone of the narrative itself. It is as if Mrs Lessing too has come to a point of stasis, not through completion, but through a weariness with a linear chronological narrative through which the story progresses but Martha does not. By this time she is struggling with the sense-making medium of realism to convey the non-sense, the irrationality and fragmented nature of Martha's personality, and the two do not fit. In other words, the traditional tools of realist fiction (omniscient viewpoint, conventional sentence structure, a chronological, causal narrative, a substantial investment in character, non-reflexive subject matter) seem inadequate to convey the complex potential of Martha's 'self', which she is trying to find, but which her author is trying to find also. By the end of *A Ripple from the Storm* Doris Lessing is frustrated with the form of the realist novel. Martha cannot 'move on' because Mrs Lessing's use of narrative techniques at this stage in her development as a novelist do not allow her to convey the dynamics and movement and growth in the psyche. The linear convention of chronological story-telling – 'and then, and then' – has to give way to other methods. Instead of moving *onwards* in order to progress, Martha has to move *inwards*. To enable this in her characters, as well as to show it, Mrs Lessing examines the whole process of writing fiction to explore the ways in which the form can imprison the potential of the content, and how it can liberate it. She does this in *The Golden Notebook* which comes between *A Ripple from the Storm* and *Landlocked*, which we shall look at in the next chapter.

When Mrs Lessing returned to the *Children of Violence* sequence with *Landlocked* in 1965, it was after she had taken the novel form apart, and although in *Landlocked* she employs a traditional realism (in the sense of fidelity to reality), it is different from the first three novels in tone and style. The narrative is more fluid, and moves easily between external and internal worlds. The sentences are longer, more explorative. There is a greater

variety of possibilities for Martha, a wider range of psychical
exploration has opened up for her. Dreams, visions, the non-
rational, the potential released by the breakdown of accepted
ways of seeing, these are now available to her to explore the
reasons for being 'landlocked'. By this time too Mrs Lessing
had become a student of Sufi, and this has had a profound
influence on all her subsequent work. Sufi is a form of mysticism
related to Islam, which developed in Persia about a thousand
years ago. It is not a prescriptive religion with a clear doctrine
or ideology, but expresses the belief that there is one unifying
truth underlying all religions. It maintains that man is capable
of achieving perfection, or oneness with God, through an
evolutionary process which can be accelerated through an
individual's capacity to transcend ordinary physical and
perceptual limitations. These limitations include adherence to
conventional systems of knowledge, and a characteristic of Sufi
is that experience, rather than pure intellect, is valued as
enlightening. 'Stop boasting of intellect and learning; for here
intellect is hampering, and learning is stupidity,' says Hakim
Jami, a fifteenth-century Sufi teacher.[24] In *Landlocked* Martha's
new understanding is not intellectual, and her strange
telepathetic and visionary experiences can be best understood in
terms of what Idries Shah calls a 'psychology' of Sufi ideas.[25]

The striking originality of Mrs Lessing's later work lies partly
in the ways she attempts to render the complex states of the
human psyche. She conveys everyday reality, but with a
tenacious insistence on simultaneously conveying the elusive,
unconscious and sometimes irrational thought processes that
accompany those day-to-day events. In this way she is both
describing and enacting in her writing her belief that there is
another dimension available to all of us if only we could shift
the perspective of our consciousness. Here is an example of this
kind of writing, which shows how concerned Doris Lessing is
with the point at which the rational mind gives way to intuition,
where, quite literally, words fail her:

> there was always a point at which anything – loving someone,
> a friendship, politics: one went over the edge into . . . but she
> did not understand into what. Neither the nature of the gulf
> nor what caused it, did she understand. But a note was

struck – and that it *would* strike could be counted on. And
after that. . . .

When they occurred, these sharp, improbable moments,
one felt as if they had nothing in common with what had
gone before; that they were of a consistency, a substance,
that were foreign. Yet later, looking back, it was always
precisely these turning points, or moments, which contained
or announced the truth – harshly and improbably, because
up till that time one had refused to acknowledge their
possibility. And afterwards, it was not the moments like
these, whose common quality was a suddenness, a dislocation,
that were wrong, faulty; but one's way of looking at what had
led up to them. (*Landlocked* Pt. 3, Ch. 2)

This passage has been quoted at length to show the awkwardness
of it: its confusing syntax, its sentences tailing off, its clumsiness;
all these stylistic features underline the difficulty of writing
about moments of non-verbal apprehension. But it also enacts
them, because what is being described is non-rational to the
extent that it eludes a conscious, linear progression of thought.
Mrs Lessing is showing Martha at the moment when her
perception of her lover Thomas changes, but without an
accumulation of rational thoughts leading up to it.

As precursors of change, Martha's dreams are very important.
In *Landlocked* she has a recurring dream to do with being
imprisoned on a high, dry plateau, unable to reach friends who
are sailing across the sea. She longs for water, and this is
symbolic of the spiritual aridity she feels, and the frustration of
being unable to leave Zambesia. She also dreams that she
inhabits a series of rooms which are furnished differently,
containing different people who must be kept separate. '[W]hat
was she waiting for, in waiting for (as she knew she did) a man?
Why, someone who would unify her elements' (Pt. 1, Ch. 1). In
Jungian terms, Martha yearns for a synthesis of her personality,
and to achieve this means becoming aware of those aspects
which have been neglected. Martha meets a man who can help
her in Thomas Stern, a Polish Jew who is a gardener, based on
a farm, but working as a 'nurseryman in the city'. A gardener,
nurturing growth in an alien environment, can also be seen as
an apt metaphor for Thomas's effect on Martha. Their feeling

for each other ends the division in Martha: 'her real nature had
been put into cold storage for precisely this' (Pt. 2, Ch. 1).
They shed façades, they explore their inner lives, they 'breakdown' for each other. And although their passionate, erotic
relationship does not last, Martha is deeply changed by Thomas.
Or perhaps not so much changed as allowed to blossom, her
latent qualities drawn out and validated by Thomas's acceptance
of her. Martha and Thomas become able to communicate
telepathically and this is described not as an esoteric
occurrence, but as a natural consequence of profound empathy
and sensitivity.

Thomas goes to live in a native village, where he appears to
have gone mad before dying there of blackwater fever. But
he has already expressed doubts about the conventional
categorisation of 'sane' and 'insane'. 'I tell you, Martha, if I see
a sane person then I know he's mad' (Pt. 2, Ch. 2). This
Laingian view is expanded by Doris Lessing in *The Four-Gated
City*. Thomas leaves a sheaf of damp, ant-eaten papers which
are eventually given to Martha to decipher. It is a difficult task,
because the unnumbered pages are scribbled all over with wild
comments in red pencil. Martha types the notes (obituaries of
native villagers, Polish poetry, recipes) and then types the red
pencilled comments on to flimsy paper which could be overlaid
on the original notes. Mrs Lessing implies that the non-sense
needs to be considered with the sense, and that it is only the
two together that make a kind of whole. Martha, not knowing
what to do with the typescript, finally takes it to England with
her, almost as an afterthought. It is Thomas's legacy to her,
and travels with her when she leaves behind her second
marriage and her outgrown political allegiances.

The final novel in the *Children of Violence* series, *The Four-Gated
City*, is very long, and spans a period of approximately fifty
years. It is a sprawling novel, where the narrative movement is
not so much linear as concentric, with Martha at the centre of
three overlapping worlds: the outside world of politics and
wars, the immediate community of the Coldridge family, and
the inner world of her expanding consciousness. Doris Lessing
shows how these three circles affect one another, and how
Martha's search for 'wholeness' has changed focus from
preceding novels. Originally Martha is concerned to merge into

a marriage, or into a political cause, to lose the egocentric self. But, by the end of *The Four-Gated City*, she realises that it is not narrowly selfish to concentrate on her own individuality, to go inward, since what is most subjective is also most universal. The dynamics of this discovery are detailed by Mrs Lessing in *The Golden Notebook*, so that if her novels are read in strictly chronological order Martha's insights have already been arrived at by a former protagonist. Here we see Martha struggling to accommodate the new perceptions she has trained herself to achieve, and by the end of the novel to use them to assist the very survival of the human race.

When Martha arrives in London at the beginning of *The Four-Gated City* we are reminded of Mrs Lessing's colonial legacy, and the viewpoint of the exile. (This novel uses much of the material documented in her non-fiction book, *In Pursuit of the English*.) It is precisely because Martha does not 'belong' that she has a very clear picture of post-war London, both physically and socially. The contrast between the real Piccadilly Circus and her colonial apprehension of it as 'the hub of the Empire' makes her laugh, and her un-English eye enables her to see gaps and inconsistencies of which the English are unaware. At first this perception is used realistically in observations about social class and the bomb-damaged city. But very soon this alien way of seeing includes Martha's visionary capacity, first encountered in *Martha Quest* when she has a mystical experience on the African veld. 'And now, into the quiet, something she had forgotten . . . that somewhere in one's mind was a wavelength, a band where music jigged and niggled, with or without words . . . the words of the songs, or the phrases, had a relevance – one could learn from them' (Pt. 1, Ch. 1). Martha also experiences a vision of a lost Golden Age through a moment of sexual intensity. These reminders of Martha's inner world come early in the novel, and are of increasing importance by the end of it, when this kind of communication becomes the norm rather than the exception.

The political and social moods of the 1940s, 1950s and 1960s are shown through the Coldridge family, from the matriarchal grand political hostess to the grandchildren living in a commune in the country. This perhaps makes the novel sound more of a social or family saga than it is. What Mrs Lessing does is to use the family as a sounding board to echo trends, movements, transitions: communism, the cold war, the shocks of Suez and Hungary in the mid 1950s, the growing disaffection with communism – these aspects of the outer world are evoked, lingered on and then dismissed. A commitment is succeeded by another commitment to something else, building up the impression of the fleeting nature not only of the loyalties of the characters, but of the ideologies, movements, causes with which they are temporarily aligned. Similarly, personal relationships are perused in detail, but the narratorial emphasis is not on their fulfilment. This is one of the ways in which Doris Lessing differs from most of her contemporaries. She does not let her novels come to rest within a resolution achieved through personal change and growth which is limited to human interaction. For her, the real change comes within the self, so that, in a sense, nothing changes except an individual's entire perspective.

In *The Four-Gated City* Martha lives in Mark Coldridge's house as his secretary, housekeeper, mistress and surrogate mother for assorted children. All these roles are given due attention by Mrs Lessing, but she does not allow Martha to find fulfilment in any of them. At certain periods during her time with Mark, Martha sees herself as the lynchpin of the household, a matron holding everything together. But she acknowledges the brevity of her power: 'luckily one never stayed in any stage long, these caravanserais were only for limited visits' (Pt. 3, Ch. 2). The word 'caravanserais' (an Eastern inn for travelling merchants or pilgrims) links us to the Sufi writer Omar Khayyám, and the stanza in his *Rubáiyát*:

> Think, in this batter'd Caravanserai
> Whose doorways are alternate Night and Day
> How Sultan after Sultan with his Pomp
> Abode his hour or two, and went his way.
> (Translation – Edward FitzGerald)

We are reminded of transience, and by eliminating political ideology (in its widest sense) and personal relationships as permanent bases to build on, Martha is pushed into examining the potentialities of the self. Thus running parallel to the social and political aspects of the novel is Martha's work on the stages of her psychical evolution.

In the course of *The Four-Gated City* Doris Lessing explores
the concept of madness, a process she began in *The Golden
Notebook* and pursues in her later novels, particularly in *Briefing
for a Descent into Hell*. She has also, by dint of going without food
and sleep over a period of time, experienced a form of madness
herself. Her ideas mesh closely with those of R. D. Laing, who
writes in *The Politics of Experience*:

> The condition of alienation, of being asleep, of being
> unconscious, of being out of one's mind, is the condition of the
> normal man.
>   Society highly values its normal man. It educates children to
> lose themselves and to become absurd, and thus to be normal.
>   Normal men have killed perhaps 100,000,000 of their fellow
> normal men in the last fifty years. (Ch. 1)

In *Children of Violence* Doris Lessing is acutely aware of this
paradox. Mark's wife Lynda (in *The Four-Gated City*) is labelled
'mad' in childhood because she has telepathic ability. Mrs
Lessing suggests that in the future our present treatment of
people with telepathic or other 'abnormal' abilities will be seen
as the equivalent of burning witches. Meanwhile, Lynda and
her kind are put in mental hospitals because they are seen as
threats to the maintenance of accepted reality. When she is not
in hospital Lynda lives in the basement of the Coldridge house,
and Martha visits her there. As Barbara Hill Rigney makes
clear, Lynda functions in this novel as a version of Bertha
Rochester, in *Jane Eyre*, but: 'As Brontë's Bertha can be seen as
Jane Eyre's mad, bad self, so Lynda can be seen as Martha's
mad, good self.'[26] Martha realises the healing potential of being
with Lynda and letting go, of daring to go 'a long way inside of
Lynda's country'.

She spends a month in the basement with Lynda, the location
being symbolic of the depths she has to plumb. Gradually, she
begins to learn Lynda's language and enters into her world. It
is an extraordinary, cathartic experience for her, rather like the
plunge into the red mud with Alice when they were both
pregnant. When she ventures outside during this period her
perspective is dramatically changed. The natural world seems
amazingly beautiful, and Martha sees it in a kind of ecstasy.
'The sky oh the sky! and the trees in the square, whose

branches moving in gentle air sent her messages of such joy, such peace, till she cried, Oh trees, I love you, and sky I love you!' (Pt. 4, Ch. 2). But with this new sensitivity of perception the human race appears disgusting. In a Swiftian apprehension of her fellow beings which recurs in Doris Lessing's novels from this point onwards, Martha not only sees them as 'half-drugged, or half asleep, dull' but also as 'defectively evolved animals'.

> For their eyes were half-useless: many wore bits of corrective glass over these spoiled or ill-grown organs; their ears were defective: many wore machines to help them hear even as much as the sounds made by their fellows: and their mouths were full of metal and foreign substances to assist teeth that were rotting . . . their guts were full of drugs because they could not defecate normally; and their nervous systems were numbed. . . . They lived in an air which was like a thick soup of petrol and fumes and stink of sweat and bad air from lungs full of the smoke they used as a narcotic, and filthy air from their bowels. (Pt. 4, Ch. 2)

In her newly awakened state Martha comes to understand that the individual consciousness is related to a collective consciousness: 'since the growing point was never, could never be, just Martha's: could not be only the property or territory of one individual' (Pt. 4, Ch. 2).

In *The Four-Gated City* Martha is forced to confront the problem of her relationship with her mother. When Mrs Quest writes from Zambesia that she is coming to London to stay with Martha she panics, and lies in bed for a week in some kind of shock. All her life she has felt unloved and rejected by her mother, and in the four earlier novels of this sequence their relationship is shown to be one of awkwardness, suspicion and resentment. Although Martha is now 35, and the source of strength and confidence for other people, the thought of her mother's visit reduces her to a needy little child, 'a small girl, inwardly weeping mamma, mamma, why are you so cold, so unkind' (Pt. 2, Ch. 3). When Mrs Quest arrives, Martha makes a tentative effort to be accepted as she is, but to no avail. Her mother disrupts the household by compulsive cleaning, and then has a breakdown during which she expresses a perverted angry view of Martha's sexuality. Martha gets her to see a psychotherapist, and after an hour of violent abuse towards her daughter, she decides to fly home the next day. Martha is never able to talk openly with her mother, or be accepted by her. Mrs Quest dies in Zambesia, and they never meet again.

The final section of *The Four-Gated City* is in the form of documents from survivors which give details of a nuclear catastrophe. Martha, Lynda and other people with extrasensory perception throughout the British Isles have foreseen the disaster, and moves are made to the West coast and to Ireland to escape the radioactivity carried by the prevailing winds. Some people are evacuated at the last minute by aircraft to other parts of the world. One of the letters amongst these documents is written by Martha, now living on an island off the West of Scotland. She tells of their struggles for survival and their primitive life on the island, and also of the children born on the island, some of whom have unusual capacities and paranormal powers. Martha recognises that: 'They don't have to be shielded from the knowledge of what the human race is in this century – they know it. I don't know how they know it. It is as if – can I put it like this? – they are beings who include that history in themselves and who have transcended it' (Appendix). The novel ends with the news that one of these children – a black child entrusted to Martha before the catastrophe – is being sent to Mark's son Francis, who is living in Nairobi, to work as a gardener. Like that of Thomas Stern, Martha's former lover, his vocation is symbolic of growth and new life. Despite the novel's concern with the legacy of violence and with the nuclear holocaust, it ends on a note of optimism. Mrs Lessing has faith in the survival of the human race, provided it manages to evolve the necessary qualities for such a survival.

Perhaps the main problem for the reader of *The Four-Gated City* is to what extent the force of the novel relies on sharing the author's beliefs. The impetus of the novel directs the reader towards an acceptance of a realm of higher consciousness. This in turn entails a different perspective on the world, so that the traditional methods of change – politics, wars, education, social policies – are shown to be ineffectual. Doris Lessing does not explicitly work at convincing her readers of the truth of her vision. As Lorna Sage points out: 'Sometimes she seems to be writing as though her audience either knows all about it already, or never will: as though – in the oldest of mystic paradoxes – there are no words, only more or less obstructive, or more or less handy, labels.'[27] In fact this technique fits in with the idea of the Sufi teaching story: the moral is not pointed; the listener either understands or not. If the time is ripe, it is implied, then there will be understanding. But I am suggesting here that whether or not one accepts Mrs Lessing's viewpoint, *Children of Violence* is a remarkable chronicle. Its scope reflects her wide range of questioning and how much she has experienced and rejected over the seventeen years of the novels' writing and publication. What is always consistent, however, and perhaps the most important aspect of the sequence, is the moment of Martha Quest's illumination in the African bush when she becomes one with the universe. In that moment she realises that 'what was futile was her own idea of herself and her place in the chaos of matter. What was demanded of her was that she should accept something quite different' (Pt. 1, Ch. 2). The 'something quite different' is what Martha struggles towards throughout the five volumes of *Children of Violence*. Her quest leads her through roles, groups, countries and causes. Finally, in *The Four-Gated City* she at last accepts that only by moving inwards will she find what she seeks. 'Here, where else, you fool, you poor fool, where else has it been, ever . . . ?' (Pt. 4, Ch. 4).

4

The Golden Notebook

The Golden Notebook was published in 1962, and is perhaps the best known of all Mrs Lessing's novels. Its publication came in the middle of the *Children of Violence* sequence, after *A Ripple from the Storm* and before *Landlocked*. Through her new protagonist, Anna Wulf, Doris Lessing explores and extends aspects of Martha Hesse; in particular, the two characters share similar feelings of alienation and division within themselves. Indeed, division and fragmentation and how they are overcome is a major theme of this novel, and one which later feeds back into the two final volumes of *Children of Violence*. One of Mrs Lessing's aims in *The Golden Notebook* is to give readers an idea of the intellectual and moral climate of Britain in the mid twentieth century, and she does this by using themes which seem to her to convey that climate. In fact, this novel was written 'before its time' in that it anticipated cultural trends (such as feminism and attitudes towards madness) which were not generally accepted until some years later. In *The Golden Notebook* Mrs Lessing reconsiders the colonial material she used in her earlier novels, but this time the focus has shifted because she examines the process of turning that material into fiction. She also looks again at Marxism, through Anna's involvement with the British Communist Party. And through her characters, she discusses the role of women in the mid century.

Politics, madness and the roles of women – all these are by now familiar Lessing themes. What is different and new about *The Golden Notebook* is its form, which itself echoes the content in its fragmentation, so that theme and form reflect each other. As was said earlier, *A Ripple from the Storm* marked the temporary exhaustion of Mrs Lessing's attempts to convey truth through traditional realism. In *The Golden Notebook* she takes the novel form apart to see how far, if at all, fiction is capable of truth-telling. One of the problems looked at in the novel is writer's block, the cessation of artistic creativity. It considers not only the psychological features of this condition, but also the technical ones. Is it possible that the form of the conventional novel can act as a block to the writer who wishes to express the irrational and the unconventional? In *The Golden Notebook* Doris Lessing acknowledges this difficulty, and sets out to free Anna's creativity through her exploration of the novel form.

'Form', the *way* in which something is said, and 'content', *what* is actually said, are always inter-related. One affects the other, although in prose this may not be so obvious as in poetry. We are perhaps so familiar with the realist novel that we barely notice its formal aspects, and we usually concentrate instead on the story. But the realist novel relies on a set of conventions which are often disguised by its highly referential language and its attempt to imitate the familiar surfaces of real life. These conventions include an omniscient viewpoint; a chronological, causal narrative with a beginning, middle and end; conventional sentence structure; a substantial investment in individual characters as knowable, and non-reflexive subject matter – that is, the realist novel seldom examines its own form, but looks outside itself to the real world. These realistic conventions are characteristic of the nineteenth-century novel, and they operate most successfully at a time when there is a generally agreed consensus about what constitutes reality.

At the turn of the century the movement known as 'Modernism' eschewed the mimetic quest of the realist novel, and veered towards self-examination. The linear narrative structure gave way to more fragmented prose, or else fluid, unorganised thoughts were expressed without formal sentence structures in a 'stream of consciousness'. The omniscient viewpoint, with its assumptions of cognisance and authority, was superseded by a multiplicity of apparently random impressions. The chronological, causal narrative was modified or abandoned and the modernist text often concentrated on a short period of time, spanning hours rather than years. Modernism embraced the non-rational, the subconscious, the uncertain, the evanescent and, moreover, insisted that these aspects of life were as true, if not more true, than the carefully constructed strata – 'slices of life' – presented by the realist novel. Doris Lessing greatly admired the nineteenth-century novel, and she began her work in the realist mode. But as she became more interested in the workings of the unconscious mind, and in Sufi, she began to question the techniques of realism: the rational, the causal delineation of experience became inadequate. What was needed was a variety of methods to convey the many layers of consciousness of her characters, and their states of breakdown and madness. In addition, she began to question the veracity of the novel; that is to say, whether or not the novel, despite its fictionality, can say something true. In the Preface Mrs Lessing explains the function of *Free Women* within *The Golden Notebook*:

> To put the short novel *Free Women* as a summary and condensation of all that mass of material, was to say something about the conventional novel, another way of describing the dissatisfaction of a writer when something is finished: 'How little I have managed to say of the truth, how little I have caught of all that complexity; how can this small neat thing be true when what I experienced was so rough and apparently formless and unshaped.' (p. 14)

Anna also writes part of her diary as factually as possible, in order to see if the plain facts are nearer to the truth than the carefully shaped material that goes into a novel. By examining the novel form so thoroughly within *The Golden Notebook* Doris Lessing made an important contribution to the post-modernist debate about the nature of fiction. Many post-modern novels are reflexive, their content being their own methodology. Doris Lessing's novels are never purely formal, however. She is deeply interested in her raw material as well as in ways of representing it, and she never loses sight of the real world. The strength and innovation of *The Golden Notebook* is the degree to which it combines both aspects: the realist story and the examination of realism.

The form of this novel is very complicated, and very carefully worked out. It contains a short, realistic novel called *Free Women*, divided into five parts. Interspersed between the sections of this novel are four extracts from four different coloured notebooks, kept by Anna, the heroine of *Free Women*: 'a black notebook, which is to do with Anna Wulf the writer; a red notebook, concerned with politics; a yellow notebook, in which

I make stories out of my experience; and a blue notebook which
tries to be a diary' (pp. 461–2). The four notebooks emphasise
the divisions in Anna's personality. It is almost as if she is four
different people, adopting a persona to suit each one. By using
the device of the notebooks, Mrs Lessing is able to convey the
variety of moods, memories, thoughts, conscious and unconscious
motives and habits that make up the individual Anna Wulf.
Time, place, memory, intersect so that the reader sees not a
coherent past that fully explains the present Anna, but rather
the muddled, sometimes contradictory skein of events and
feelings which may never amount to an adequate explanation of
her. Finally, there is also a golden-coloured notebook, in which
Anna and her lover give each other sentences to begin a new
novel. Anna's is the first sentence of *Free Women*, thus linking
the end of the notebooks to the beginning of the novel *The
Golden Notebook*. The fragmentary structure of the novel is
thereby unified, and turned into a circular, coherent whole.

The fragmented form of *The Golden Notebook* has quite a
dislocating effect on the reader. It jolts us from total immersion
in the narrative, since the realist novel within the text, *Free
Women*, is interrupted by other material. We are not allowed to
settle down for long. By showing us other aspects of Anna, her
past in Africa, her political involvements, her writer's block,
her psychotherapy, it makes us realise the inadequacy of
traditional realism to cope without all this complexity without
somehow fictionalising it, making it smooth and malleable. In
addition, through Anna's attempts to organise such disparate
material into *her* fiction (the novel she is writing in the yellow
notebook), we are shown the steps involved in such a process:
selection, omission, shaping and falsifying. For example, one of
the central episodes in *The Golden Notebook*, a woman being
rejected by a man after a long relationship, is treated in several
different ways. In *Free Women* we learn of the event after it has
happened, and that three years later Anna has not really
recovered from it. In the blue notebook (Anna's diary) she
writes in great detail of the day in 1954 when Michael leaves
her. Dissatisfied with that account, she rewrites the day in
laconic, factual sentences so that all the pain becomes reduced
to 'I realised that Michael had finally decided to break it off. I
must pull myself together' (p. 361). In the yellow notebook
(Anna's novel) the episode is rewritten in fictional form, so that

Anna becomes Ella, and Michael becomes Paul. In the yellow notebook there are also synopses of short stories, reworking the same theme. These different perspectives on the same event allow the reader to see the many ways the raw material can be represented.

In *The Golden Notebook* Mrs Lessing refuses the role of tactful mediator between her material and her reader, for so long the traditional role of the woman novelist, particularly when dealing with controversial themes. She deliberately leaves some of the material unpalatable and unconvincing. She reveals to us both the events of Anna's life, and the various ways of recording them, all of which are shown to be only partially true, even the most factual and unvarnished. But all these attempts bring us, time and time again, up against a central artistic problem that traditional novels attempt most vigorously to disguise: the inability of realism to convey reality. Anna says, in effect, 'No, it wasn't like that, or like that' but instead of trying to cover the gap between experience and its representation Mrs Lessing draws our attention to it repeatedly, almost puritanically. It is as if she needs to do so in order to convince herself of her own integrity; that by showing the reader the mechanics of fiction-making, she is thereby acquitted of falsehood.

The disconnected form of *The Golden Notebook* points continually to its own divisions, its lack of a carefully smoothed-out synthesis. Even at the end questions are left unanswered, solutions withheld. Yet it is very difficult for the reader to rest with its disorder. When we are forced to confront fragmentation, we realise our propensity to suspend disbelief, to lose ourselves in fictions. Our own longings for integration are highlighted, and like Anna's avid readers of *Frontiers of War* we will accept that 'terrible lying nostalgia' (p. 82), or any other palliative, to fulfil them. For example, we as readers know perfectly well that Anna's novel about Ella and Paul is not true, its status is self-proclaimed fiction. Nevertheless, it is very easy to become involved in the plot, to identify with the characters, to respond, in short, as if Anna the author were not also bound up in the pages of the larger text, *The Golden Notebook*.

Within *The Golden Notebook* the novel *Free Women* is an account of two women friends living in London in the 1950s. Anna is divorced and has a small daughter, Janet. She has also been rejected by her lover after a five-year relationship. Molly is divorced and has a son of 20 called Tommy. Both women have been members of the Communist Party, and both have had psychotherapy from the same analyst. Anna keeps four notebooks of different colours to record different aspects of her experience. One day Tommy reads these notebooks, and accuses Anna of dishonesty, of pretending things are not chaotic when in reality they are. 'I don't think there's a pattern anywhere – you are just making patterns, out of cowardice' (p. 273). During the course of *Free Women*, Tommy tries to commit suicide and succeeds in blinding himself instead. Anna quarrels with a homosexual couple living in part of her flat, and asks them to leave. Her daughter, at her own request, goes to a girls' boarding school. Left alone, Anna begins to have a breakdown, to go mad. She has an affair with an American, recovers, and begins to do welfare work and marriage guidance. Molly remarries. It is only at the end of *The Golden Notebook* that we learn that Anna has written *Free Women* out of the raw material of her life, collected in her diary.

This brisk summary of the plot reflects the tone of the novel. *Free Women* is written in the third person, and its tone is objective, and somewhat detached. The emotional and non-rational elements associated with the events are separated from them, and are written about in the Blue Notebook, leaving *Free Women* as an ironic and desiccated version of the truth. Doris Lessing, is, to some extent, parodying the conventional realist novel, and by its flatness allows us to see how the chaos and vitality of the notebooks has indeed been structured, but in the process, diminished. The notebooks (apart from the golden-coloured notebook) each finish in various kinds of frustration, whereas *Free Women* achieves an ending. But by its sensible, chronological narrative and its refusal to incorporate frustration, it is finally dissatisfying. Without the juxtaposition of the notebooks to flesh it out, *Free Women* would be dry and skeletal. Yet it plays an integral part in *The Golden Notebook* as a whole, elaborately echoing and prefiguring essential themes. During the reading of *The Golden Notebook* we involuntarily supplement the text of *Free Women* with our knowledge of events and moods from the notebooks, so that as readers we rebuild the process of fictionalisation that Doris Lessing painstakingly breaks down. Our experience of reading a novel is usually linear, but in *The*

Golden Notebook we are constantly forced to re-examine linearity by being presented with stratal or cylical arrangements of the same 'objective' events.

The black notebook is originally divided into two columns, one headed 'Source' and the other 'money'. In it Anna deals with the material she used to write a best-selling novel, *Frontiers of War*, and with her consequent literary success. (This is a rewritten version of the material Doris Lessing used in the early volumes of *Children of Violence*.) We see the insistent world of agents, television adaptations and film rights, and Mrs Lessing includes some very funny parodies in this section. As Anna loses her ability to write, the black notebook becomes a cuttings file for new items about violence in Africa. The red notebook is mainly to do with Anna's experiences with the British Communist Party from 1950–7, her growing unease with it, and her final extrication from it. Like the black notebook, the red one becomes full of newspaper cuttings, again about violence. The yellow notebook begins with a novel Anna is writing, called *The Shadow of the Third*, and her comments on the process of writing it. This is a fictionalised version of her own life, and the juxtaposition of it with *Free Women* enables the reader to see how Anna selects and shapes and reconstructs the material for the purposes of fiction. To add to the seemingly infinite reflexiveness of *The Golden Notebook*, Ella, the heroine of Anna's novel, is herself writing a novel about suicide. The yellow notebook includes ideas for short stories, parodies and pastiche, the last being symptomatic of Anna's writer's block. The blue notebook functions as Anna's diary, a deliberate attempt not to turn everything into fiction, but to try to keep a factual account of what happens in her life. In it she records her writer's block, her sessions with her psychotherapist, the ending of her love affair with Michael, her work for the Communist Party, her relationship with Molly and with her own daughter. Most important, it describes her breakdown in some detail, and her affair with an American, Saul Green. Sometimes the diary entries are short and factual, sometimes longer and reflective. The blue notebook is the most detailed account we have of Anna's life and it is, in effect, the one that we as readers have to rely on. *Free Women* and *The Shadow of the Third* are fictionalised versions of Anna's life, and the blue notebook, with its status of diary, gives it a veracity the other versions lack.

Finally, in the golden-coloured notebook, Anna synthesises the various experiences kept separate in the other notebooks, so that they approximate to a kind of wholeness of vision. And attaining this integration enables her to begin to write again.

The notebooks are kept as Anna's way of making sense of the world, and by separating the various strands and aspects of her life in this way she hopes to impose a pattern on chaos. In all the notebooks, at some time, she is unable to continue writing, and they become a dumb record of her blocked creativity – scrapbooks merely of newspaper cuttings or jottings of plots and scenarios. It proves impossible to keep events coherent and separate, and the notebooks are in themselves a record of that failure. At one point in the yellow notebook Anna says: 'This sort of comment belongs to the blue notebook, not this one' (p. 520). When she is able to abandon the separate notebooks, the golden notebook becomes all that is needed to record her perceptions. Because she has allowed herself to break down and allow the chaos in, she is able to achieve a final integration.

Doris Lessing may not have welcomed the categorisation of *The Golden Notebook* as a feminist text, but nevertheless in 1962 it was a very important statement about women's roles. Far from being a celebration of women's independence from men, however, the novel explores relations between men and women, and the seemingly inescapable female need for the opposite sex. The relationships described are usually troubled and abrasive, but running throughout the novel as a kind of unmentioned (or unmentionable) subtext is the idea of a woman, living happily with her husband, sexually and emotionally fulfilled by him, cooking for him and bearing his children. I think it is important not to see *The Golden Notebook* as a purely feminist novel simply because of the women's dissatisfaction with men, since this interpretation means ignoring many of the things Doris Lessing is actually saying. Time and again Anna, or her counterpart Ella, express very unfeminist needs. What is important to them is not to be liberated *from* marriage, but to enhance the *quality* of marriage. The men they meet are emotionally stupid, unaware of the negative effect they have on women. Ella 'thinks for the hundredth time that in their emotional life all these intelligent men use a level so much lower than anything they use for work, that they might be different creatures' (p. 445).

The Golden Notebook broke new ground in its open discussion of female sexuality from the point of view of a woman writer. Ella compares the vaginal and clitoral orgasm, and insists that the former is possible only with a man she loves. When Paul says 'Do you know that there are eminent physiologists who say women have no physical basis for vaginal orgasm?' Ella replies 'Then they don't know much, do they?' (p. 220). While Paul and Ella love each other their sex life is good, but it changes as the relationship deteriorates. After Paul leaves, Ella sleeps with men who do not satisfy her. This is partly because she does not love them, but also because they are poor lovers. There is a great deal about men's sexual inadequacies in this book, from lovers who are technically efficient but emotionally detached, to those who are simple inept. What Mrs Lessing reiterates is the different nature of the sexual act for a woman if it is in the context of love. Promiscuity is not a solution for either Anna or Ella, and they mock the notion of their 'freedom'.

> 'Free,' says Julia. 'Free! What's the use of us being free if they aren't? I swear to God, that every one of them, even the best of them, have the old idea of good women and bad women. And what about us? Free, we say, yet the truth is they get erections when they're with a woman they don't give a damn about, but we don't have an orgasm unless we love him. What's free about that?'. (p. 446)

After Paul leaves, Ella is tormented by sexual desire. She is distressed because it is not for any specific person, but then she realises that this desire is fed by a myriad of emotional hungers, and that 'when she loved a man again, she would return to normal . . . a woman's sexuality is, so to speak, contained by a man, if he is a real man; she is, in a sense, put to sleep by him, she does not think about sex' (p. 443). This line of thought means that Ella has to depend on a man for her completion, a dangerous dependence in this novel since there is not a 'real man' in it. We are not shown the enriching aspects of Ella's relationship with Paul, or those of Anna's relationship with Michael. Neither of these men, or the women's subsequent lovers, emerge as attractive or likeable characters. Mrs Lessing herself seems unaware that she has drawn these men so savagely. In an interview after the book was published, the interviewer says: 'your male characters in that book are really very unpleasant, all of them. There isn't a good male character.' Mrs Lessing replies: 'I don't think that's true . . . I think the male characters are terrific.'[28] This seems an extraordinary thing to say, since in the novel itself she gives them very few redeeming features.

Along with women's dependence on men in this novel is shown the devastating effect of being rejected by them, and the passivity with which this is accepted. Fear of breakdown is always very close to Anna and Ella, and the loss of a relationship brings that fear closer. When Michael leaves her Anna knows that 'an awful black whirling chaos is just outside me, waiting to move into me' (p. 360). To avoid this, the women in *The Golden Notebook* continue the passive behaviour shown by Martha in the first three volumes of *Children of Violence*. Their instinct to boost the morale of men is very powerful, and for all their intelligence, the women in *The Golden Notebook* seldom assert themselves on their own behalf. The women support each other against the pain caused by men, and to help get over it they make brave jokes about survival. But Anna has the thought that some things may be so bad that they can never be got over: 'Because when I really face it I don't think I've really got over Michael. I think it's done for me' (p. 70). It seems impossible for the women in *The Golden Notebook* to envisage their lives without men, yet the price they feel they have to pay to keep a man, in terms of compromise and deception, is too high for them. But even so they constantly recognise their willingness to sacrifice themselves, to become the passive acquiescent woman. In her relationship with Paul Ella realises that, in Jungian terms, she is using only one side of her character but, unusually, she has hidden her 'good' side: 'I have as a shadow a good woman, grown-up and strong and un-asking. Which means I am using with him my "negative" self' (p. 213). She hides her writing from him because he does not like her doing it; at one point she even admits that she was prepared to give it up entirely. 'Suppose Paul had said to me: I'll marry you if you promise never to write another word? My God, I would have done it!' (p. 311). Mrs Lessing states, through Ella, that women's emotions are made to seem anachronistic in present day society, and have not evolved to fit notions of separateness and independence. *The Golden Notebook* is

not a treatise advocating autonomy for women; rather, it is a
lament for its seeming impossibility.

Towards the end of the novel, in the golden notebook section,
Anna realises that she is not the victim of men so much as of
herself. When a lover asks her 'do I really give you such a bad
time?' Anna, after hours of psychotherapy, is able to say 'I
haven't done time with the witch-doctors not to know that no
one does anything to me. I do it to myself' (p. 599). But this is
only after she is able to accept the liberating effects of breaking
down, and has abandoned the attempt to keep chaos at a
safe distance by using her notebooks as safe, separating
compartments.

Splitting and fragmentation recur as themes in *The Golden
Notebook*, and not only in the field of emotional relationships.
Anna joins the Communist Party because of 'a need for
wholeness, for an end to the split, divided, unsatisfactory way
we all live' (p. 171). But she comes to realise that the split is in
fact intensified, since the theory and objectives of the party are
so at odds with the real world. And even within herself, she
recognises at least two political personalities: one is detached
and wise, the other a party fanatic. Anna's initial commitment
to the Communist Party aggravates her guilt at being a writer.
'Little novels about the emotions' (p. 61) are sneered at, since
they are to do with the individual, and not the communal.
Anna, on one level, knows that the subjective can also be
universally true: 'If Marxism means anything, it means that a
little novel about the emotions should reflect "what's real"
since the emotions are a function and a product of a society'
(p. 61). On another level, she is paralysed by guilt at her own
indulgence:

> at that moment I sit down to write, someone comes into the
> room, looks over my shoulder, and stops me. . . . It could be
> a Chinese peasant. Or one of Castro's guerilla fighters. Or an
> Algerian fighting in the F.L.N. Or Mr. Mathlong. They
> stand here in the room and they say, why aren't you doing
> something about us, instead of wasting your time scribbling?
> (p. 614)

Anna leaves the Communist Party as the same time as Michael
leaves her. Earlier in the year she has finished a long period of

psychotherapy. Without three of her closest involvements, Anna leaves herself open and vulnerable to the impact of new experiences. Almost consciously, she is 'clearing the decks' to allow space for the next phase of her life. In the yellow notebook Anna allows her character Ella to recognise the potentiality of what may seem like an arid self-awareness: 'I've got to accept the patterns of self-knowledge which mean unhappiness or at least a dryness. But I can twist it into victory. A man and a woman – yes. Both at the end of their tether. Both cracking up because of a deliberate attempt to transcend their own limits. And out of the chaos, a new kind of strength' (p. 454). In the blue notebook Anna writes 'What is happening is something new in my life. I think many people have a sense of shape, of unfolding, in their lives' (p. 465).

Throughout *The Golden Notebook* we have seen Anna's devices to protect herself against breaking down: her notebooks, her roles as a conscientious party worker, a good mother, a compliant mistress. In the blue notebook Anna writes a very detailed account of a day in her life, 15 September 1954. She does this to counter Michael's criticism that because she is a writer she does not know what is true and what is fiction. This day – a kind of Joycean 'Bloomsday' – is at the centre of *The Golden Notebook*. In her account Anna writes down the minutiae of her day: giving attention to her child and to her lover, planning and preparing meals, coping with menstruation, having long discussions at the office. It is one of the most painful and claustrophobic passages in the novel, indeed in contemporary fiction. It describes the lot of countless women, and perhaps its power comes from its very ordinariness which, written about, given permanence, forces the reader to realise how appalling was a fairly typical day in the life of a woman in the mid twentieth century. Anna Wulf is shown swamped by the roles of mistress, mother, colleague and friend. She herself ceases to exist. Like the heroine of a nineteenth-century novel all her experiences are relative to other people, and her capacity for self-sacrifice and self-effacement seems limitless.

Anna's psychotherapist has restored her capacity to feel pain, and gradually her defences against it disappear. During the account of 15 September we realise that the juggling act involved in keeping everyone happy cannot continue indefinitely. Anna resigns from her job, her lover leaves, and her daughter goes to boarding school. Her roles suddenly disappear and she is left to be Anna Wulf, without the protective covering of the defences she has hitherto considered essential to maintain. When Janet goes to boarding school Anna is freed from the routine of being a mother, and realises that 'An Anna is coming to life that died when Janet was born' (p. 531). She lets a room in her flat to an American, Saul Green, who is, in conventional terms, unbalanced, and falls in love with him. Influenced by him, she allows herself to break down.

Words have been Anna's link to sanity, and significantly during her breakdown they begin to lose their meaning: 'the words swim and have no sense and I am conscious only of me, Anna, as a pulse in a great darkness, and the words that I, Anna, write down are nothing, or like the secretions of a caterpillar that are forced out in ribbons to harden in the air' (p. 463). Words fail her, literally. They are no longer adequate to describe how she feels or what she knows from her disintegration: 'The people who have been there, in the place in themselves where words, patterns, order, dissolve, will know what I mean and the others won't' (p. 609). Instead, visual images take over, and Anna acknowledges in her dreams what she has called the 'Joy-in-spite principle'. This originally took the form of a maliciously smiling crocodile in her dreams, and now assumes the persona of Saul, on whom Anna is projecting the cruel side of her nature. Finally, through a dream where Saul and Anna are together, she acknowledges that she, too, embodies the sadistic qualities of 'joy-in-destruction', and this acceptance of her darkest side gives her great peace on awakening. In a further dream she is taken through her past as if a projectionist were showing her a film, and 'there was a fusion, instead of seeing separate scenes, people, faces, movements, glances, they were all together' (p. 611). And at the end of it, Anna realises that 'the reason why I have only given my attention to the heroic or the beautiful or the intelligent is because I won't accept that injustice and the cruelty, and so won't accept the small endurance that is bigger than anything' (p. 611). Claiming the reality of her own nature – its cruelty as well as its altruism – has enabled Anna to accept its universality, and to recognise the heroism of everyday courage.

Saul both initiates and echoes Anna's symptoms of madness.

She is sometimes able to predict his actions or to read his thoughts, and she realises that she is often expressing his illness for him. As Doris Lessing explains in the 'Preface' to *The Golden Notebook* 'Anna and Saul Green the American "break down". They are crazy, lunatic, mad – what you will. They "break down" into each other, into other people, break through the false patterns they have made of their pasts, the patterns and formulas they have made to shore up themselves and each other, dissolve' (p. 7). As Anna comes through the process of breakdown and disintegration she abandons her four separate notebooks, and uses a new, golden-coloured notebook to record the experience of breaking-though. The need to keep events separate has been overtaken by the chaos that she has succumbed to, and by the knowledge she has achieved from it. The worst – and the best – has happened, and the defences are no longer needed. The golden notebook acts as a symbol of Anna's psychic integration, just as the previous four notebooks symbolised her feelings of disunity. Saul and Anna give each other sentences for a new novel, and Anna's sentence is 'The two women were alone in the London flat' which is of course the first sentence of *Free Women*.

The deliberate banality of the last section of *Free Women* which ends *The Golden Notebook* does not undermine Anna's triumph. Her new psychic health does not change the world, and her aspirations are shown to be low key. Paul tells Ella in the yellow notebook, and Anna tells Saul in the golden notebook, that they are 'boulder-pushers'. Sisyphus-like, their task is to push a great boulder (representing truth intuitively recognised) up the high mountain of human stupidity. Every so often it rolls down, almost to the bottom, and the boulder-pushers begin again. This image of perpetual effort with the prospect of very little achievement replaces Anna's idealistic communist dreams. World change, by the end of the novel, becomes a local, almost a domestic affair, first involving change in an individual. Great theories and answers are abandoned, and small hopeful images remain. During her time with her psychotherapist, Mrs Marks, Anna is exasperated by her insistence on the necessity of feeling a wide range of emotions. Anna says that even after a nuclear holocaust Mrs Marks will think of the first tentative blades of grass growing out of the lava in a million years time. Anna is irritated by this tenacity of hope, but after her acceptance of the power of 'small endurance' the image returns to her mind. *The Golden Notebook*, concerned with some of the most vociferous causes of our time, does not finally allow any of them to come up with the answers. We are left with the 'small endurance' and a tentative blade of grass.

The Golden Notebook is a very long, intensely rich book, and it is not surprising that it has been seized on as a polemic by various movements. At the end of the 1971 'Preface' Mrs Lessing concedes that a writer should not require the reader to receive a novel exactly as it is written, and goes on to say: 'the book is alive and potent and fructifying and able to promote thought and discussion *only* when its plan and shape and intention are not understood, because that moment of seeing the shape and plan and intention is also the moment when there isn't any more to be got out of it' (p. 22). For many people, including myself, the experience and reading and re-reading *The Golden Notebook* over the years is that of absorbing several different novels. Our responses vary according to our own processes of growth and changing perceptions. We may see communism, feminism or mysticism as the main theme of the novel. For Mrs Lessing, it acted as a bridge between realism and the kind of writing (mythopoeic, metaphoric, mystical) she felt was needed to convey experiences beyond the range of traditional realism. After *The Golden Notebook* she is able, with great confidence, to use realism as only one form of communication in fiction. The final two volumes of *Children of Violence*, and several subsequent novels, owe their originality in this respect to the experimentation of *The Golden Notebook*. Freed through her courageous examination of the novel form (it was brave because what if for her fiction *had* proved to be merely lies?) Doris Lessing goes on to chart the inner space we all inhabit.

5

Madness, Dreams and Prophecy

The Golden Notebook was a radical examination of the novel form, and Mrs Lessing's subsequent novels incorporate the lessons she learnt from it, namely the inadequacy of realism to convey non-rational, non-logical modes of thought and experience. Thus, in *Landlocked*, Thomas Stern's crazy, semi-legible manuscript lies at the centre of the novel, its apparent meaninglessness deliberately made more significant than the realist text which surrounds it. *The Four-Gated City* continues the Laingian hypothesis that so-called madness and dreams may be states of greater perception than so-called sanity and wakefulness. This theory becomes central to Mrs Lessing's next three novels – *Briefing for a Descent into Hell, The Summer Before the Dark* and *The Memoirs of a Survivor* – where she abandons realism as and when she needs to. I think it is important to understand that she uses the fantastic, the mythic, the archetypal and the symbolic not merely as literary devices to alert us to the paucity of realism, but because she genuinely needs those modes of expression to convey her experiences of another dimension than that of the everyday world. In other words, she is not making an aesthetic point merely, like many post-modernist writers; rather, she is enlarging her technical range to cope with her expanded consciousness of what constitutes reality.

In an interview with C. J. Driver, Doris Lessing talks about her awareness of the paranormal:

I have been involved steadily in mental illness, either by knowing psychiatrists very well indeed (which is a euphemism for saying I had a long affair with one), or by being involved with people who were nuts; . . . I described that process at the end of *Four Gated City* (*sic*) how somebody is classified as mad because she has paranormal capacities. When I had finished that book, I had incredible letters from people who had been in looney bins – and who had got out, because they had stopped telling the truth, who had gone to doctors to say, 'My voices have gone', and so on . . . my view now is that we all of us all the time use capacities which science says don't exist; we couldn't exist for five minutes without them. It's not at all a question of a few extraordinary people having these capacities – we communicate with them all the time; I'm sure of that. And what is exciting is that all the modern research is coming to the same conclusion. We're just on the verge of a complete revolution in how we make sense of things.'[29]

In *Briefing for a Descent into Hell* Mrs Lessing describes the experiences of a man called Charles Watkins who is labelled mad and put into a mental hospital. As several critics, including Marion Vlastos and Roberta Rubenstein have pointed out,[30] his subsequent mental voyage has parallels with that described by Laing in *The Politics of Experience*. In that book he records a real psychotic episode of ten days in the life of a man called Jesse Watkins. Laing calls it 'A Ten-Day Voyage', and describes the potential of such a journey in a way that is very close to the experience of Mrs Lessing's character, Charles Watkins.

The person who has entered this inner realm (if only he is allowed to experience this) will find himself going, or being conducted – one cannot clearly distinguish active from passive here – on a journey.

This journey is experienced as going further 'in', as going back through one's personal life, in and back and through and beyond into the experience of all mankind, of the primal man, of Adam and perhaps even further into the being of animals, vegetables and minerals.

In this journey there are many occasions to lose one's way, for confusion, partial failure, even final shipwreck: many terrors, spirits, demons to be encountered, that may or may not be overcome. (*The Politics of Experience*, Ch. 5)

This is a very useful description to set alongside *Briefing for a*

Descent into Hell, since it is virtually a summary of the novel itself.

During his real psychotic journey Jesse Watkins discovers that he has supernatural powers, such as the ability to heal a deep cut on his finger by simply concentrating on it. He says: 'I felt that I had sort of – um – tapped powers that in some vague way I had felt I had, or everybody had' (*The Politics of Experience*, Ch. 7). These superhuman potentialities are frequently described in esoteric literature, and in his book *Myths, Dreams and Mysteries* Mircea Eliade shows how common they are amongst primitive peoples, and throughout all religions. What Laing calls 'hyper-sanity, not sub-sanity' (*The Politics of Experience*, Ch. 7) is deeply interesting to Mrs Lessing. It links with her involvement with Sufi and its emphasis on the individual's capacity for transcendence. In an 'Afterword' to *Briefing for a Descent into Hell* she quotes from Blake's *Marriage of Heaven and Hell*:

> How do you know but ev'ry Bird that cuts the airy way
> Is an immense world of delight, clos'd by your senses five?

Her work from *The Golden Notebook* onwards begins to explore the human potential to enter into 'an immense world of delight', or at least into another world than this, by apprehending the experience described by the Sufi poet quoted by Mrs Lessing at the beginning of the novel:

> If yonder raindrop should its heart disclose,
> Behold therein a hundred seas displayed.
> In every atom, if thou gaze aright,
> Thousands of reasoning beings are contained.
> (The Sage Mahmoud Shabistari, in the fourteenth-
> century *The Secret Garden*)

This links with what Blake describes in 'Auguries of Innocence':

> To see a World in a Grain of Sand
> And a heaven in a Wild Flower,
> Hold infinity in the palm of your hand
> And Eternity in an hour.

Charles Watkins's journey, like that of Jesse Watkins, changes

his perceptions of time and space, so that his experience echoes
that of the poets. Indeed, it is an experience that lends itself to
poetic rather than prosaic exposition, since it goes beyond
linear or logical thought-processes.

Mrs Lessing uses Charles Watkins's mental journey as an
allegory of the evolution of the human condition. During it he
moves from a state of innocence to a knowledge of evil, and an
acceptance of his active involvement in it. After this he is able
to transcend his humanity, but is then sent back to earth to act
as a teacher, a reminder that mankind is not a separate entity,
but part of a whole cosmic community. Charles's journey begins
with a long sea voyage with eleven friends. Their ship is visited
by a shining, crystalline disc which takes away everyone on the
ship except Charles. After much journeying he eventually lands
on a friendly shore, and his emergence from sea to land echoes
this evolutionary step in pre-history: 'And now leaving the sea
where I have been around and around for so many centuries
my mind is ringed with Time like the deposits on shells or the
fall of years on tree trunks, I step up on the dry salty sand, with
a shake of my whole body like a wet dog' (p. 39). He feels
welcome, 'as if this was a country where hostility or dislike had
not yet been born' (p. 40). It is, Mrs Lessing seems to suggest,
a prelapserian state where fruit is abundant and wild animals
are friendly. The image of the Golden Age is again evoked, as it
was in *Children of Violence*. After a painful and difficult journey,
analogous to the birth process (as if, in this section of the novel,
Charles is re-enacting both the evolution of the collective
consciousness, and his own personal development) he finally
climbs through a narrow chasm to a plateau. Here he discovers
the ruins of a deserted city. Like the Utopian city in *Children of
Violence*, this city has a mandala at its heart, a central square
containing a circle. Charles knows that he has to prepare this
circle by cleaning away the earth and grass growing on it.
When he has done this he falls under the malign influence of
the moon. He watches a vast herd of white cattle grazing
peacefully on a plain near the city, and sees one of them killed.
He understands that his presence in this land has brought evil
into it: 'And now I understood my fall away from what I had
been when I landed, only three weeks before, into a land which
had never known killing' (p. 60). This version of the fall of man
brings Charles profound grief, and he experiences fear for the

first time since he landed. To his horror he sees three women who are familiar to him (named after three women in his everyday life) and three boys, sitting around a fire, shrieking and laughing and eating hunks of half-raw meat, drunk on blood. A dead baby lies on a heap of meat. Charles joins in this savagery, and his awareness of evil becomes a knowledge of his own potential for participation in it.

In the morning Charles walks as far from the scene as he can, so that he is too late to rejoin the women when the moon rises. By exercising free will, by moving away from the bloody orgy, Charles saves himself from temptation. But he has not reached the state of enlightenment necessary to join the crystal disc next time it comes to the city centre: 'it . . . belonged to a level of existence that my eyes were not evolved enough to see' (p. 68). The city becomes over-run with a hideous species of rat-dogs, which Mrs Lessing uses as analogous to mankind. They are permanently obsessed with sex and vicious fighting. After witnessing a dreadful battle, Charles is led by a great white bird to the square, which he clears of dead bodies and cleans with water and aromatic branches. Charles's involvement with the intense evil within himself has been prefigured in *The Golden Notebook* by Anna's encounter with the Self Hater, and in *The Four-Gated City* by Martha's deliberate exploration of her own character, 'to do with sadism, masochism, the pleasure in hurting' (p. 553), which leads her to a temporary but ultimately healing madness. Mrs Lessing repeatedly suggests in her novels that this awareness is a necessary stage of self-knowledge; a capacity for evil is the shadow side of a capacity for good. Charles is taken up by the crystal on its next visit to the city, and he sees the planet earth beneath him, a 'connecting feeding mesh' (p. 96) linking all humanity. His thoughts about the need for unity and wholeness are central to this novel, and indeed, germane to Mrs Lessing's entire canon: 'Some sort of divorce there has been somewhere along the long path of this race of man between the "I" and the "We", some sort of terrible falling away' (p. 103). Science is attacked for its unholistic view of life: 'In fact, the distinguishing feature of this new religion, and why it has proved so inadequate, is its insistence on dividing off, compartmenting, pigeon-holing' (p. 121). The attraction of Sufi is its refusal to separate areas of experience, its insistence on connections and fusion.

Charles is appointed an emissary to earth, a notion taken up later in *Canopus in Argos: Archives*. Indeed, Mrs Lessing has said that *Briefing for a Descent into Hell* is really the first volume of the *Canopus* novels. Charles's task, with others like him, is to be 'an assisting of the Earth's people through the coming Planetary Emergency in which all life may be lost' (p. 123). To this end Charles has to be reborn, an experience Doris Lessing once underwent under the influence of mescaline. She describes the process in an interview, and says that she, as the baby, felt 'a sort of cosmic boredom. This baby had been born many times before, and the mere idea of "having to go through it all over again" . . . exhausted it in advance.'[31] In *Briefing for a Descent into Hell* Charles's childhood perceptions are juxtaposed with adult strictures of what constitutes good behaviour, mostly to do with going to sleep and being placid. But at the back of his mind the child Charles knows that he has to remember something. This section of the novel closely resembles Wordsworth's *Intimations of Immortality*, which is a poetic version of the same theory:

> Our birth is but a sleep and a forgetting:
> The Soul that rises with us, our life's Star,
> Hath had elsewhere its setting,
> And cometh from afar:
> Not in entire forgetfulness,
> And not in utter nakedness,
> But trailing clouds of glory do we come
> From God, who is our home:
> Heaven lies about us in our infancy!
> Shades of the prison-house begin to close
> Upon the growing boy,
> But he beholds the light, and whence it flows,
> He sees it in his joy;
> The youth, who daily farther from the east
> Must travel, still is Nature's priest,
> And by the vision splendid
> Is on his way attended;
> At length the man perceives it die away
> And fade into the light of common day.

When Charles wakes, his long psychic journey is over, and he is in the ward of a mental hospital. Later he remembers an episode in Yugoslavia during the Second World War which, it later becomes clear, did not happen to him but to a friend and fellow soldier. Mrs Lessing seems to be implying here, as she earlier stated openly in *The Golden Notebook*, that there is no such thing as an isolated individual experience, and she demonstrates this by making Charles capable of incorporating another person's history into his own memory.

Charles finally agrees to electro-convulsive therapy in the hope that it might help him to remember something he feels 'has to do with time running out' (p. 247). From the information given to us earlier we realise that he has a mission on earth to alert people to an awareness of approaching disaster. But when he has the treatment, his ordinary memory has gone. His tone is prosaic, matter-of-fact, and the reader is left in no doubt that something vital for the survival of humanity has disappeared for ever.

In the course of this novel there is a long letter to Charles from a woman called Rosemary Baines. In it she describes having attended a lecture on education given by Charles, and during it experiencing a sense of remembering something important, long forgotten.

> It was the feeling of the quality of what you said. It went with recognition, as if I had been reminded of something I knew very well. I was possessed with a low simmering fear that I would forget again, let go – what I had been as a child. . . .
>
> But I *was* remembering. It was as if, in any moment of the day that I chose to revive it, there was a bridge across from that heightened moment when you were saying things about the children, about all of us, and the pulse of the time I was in (pp. 153–4).

In her letter Rosemary tells Charles about a friend of hers called Frederick Larson, who is an archaeologist. Frederick (like Charles, and like Anna Wulf in *The Golden Notebook*) developed a stammer at a stage in his life where he had ceased to believe in what he was saying. The stammer thus became an outward symptom of his internal doubts. Both Rosemary and Frederick recognise another realm of existence which lies behind everyday reality, tantalisingly near and yet elusive. Frederick's conventional theories about archaeology are shattered by this kind of extra understanding, and while he is lecturing his mind formulates a stream of words which propound theories opposite to those he articulates. Mrs Lessing introduces these two characters to show that they share the same awareness as Charles of humanity's extraordinary potential.

Of all Doris Lessing's novels, *Briefing for a Descent into Hell* is perhaps the one where she is at least concerned to be persuasive, to make her message palatable. There is a kind of urgency about it which reflects Charles' sense of urgency about his mission. In this novel Mrs Lessing is herself giving a warning about the fate of the planet Earth, and the need to develop new modes of listening and communication if we are to divert or transcend disaster. If one responds to this novel as an encoded signal, it then becomes a potent communication to a whole network of believers in the 'New Age', which, as Marilyn Ferguson puts it in *The Aquarian Conspiracy*, 'sees us as stewards of all our resources, inner and outer. It says that we are *not* victims, not pawns, not limited by conditions or conditioning. Heirs to evolutionary riches, we are capable of imagination, invention and experiences we have only glimpsed' (p. 30).[32] What Mrs Lessing is concerned to convey in *Briefing for a Descent into Hell* is the necessity of a holistic approach to living that takes account of both the external, everyday life, and the internal psychic life of a character. Both, she insists, are valid, have meaning, should be taken into account. In a conversation with one of his doctors Charles says 'Is that it? your dreams or your life. But it is not *or*, that is the point. It is *and*. Everything is. Your dreams *and* your life' (p. 142). Dreams, madness, the irrational: Mrs Lessing increasingly sees these elements as carrying messages that must be attended to. Often, what they say runs counter to what is happening in everyday life, and it is then, Mrs Lessing suggests, that they particularly demand attention. Charles Watkins finally turns his mind away from such disturbing intrusions. Rosemary Baines and Frederick Larson listen out for them, welcome them, and incorporate them into their conscious awareness. Quietly, they recognise and recruit people of the New Age. Charles's final, tragic rationality is warmly welcomed by his family and colleagues. Its terrible irony is left unstated.

In *The Summer Before the Dark* Doris Lessing returns to a realistic mode, but the narrative is paralleled by a dream sequence which is given as much weight as the realistic story. A middle-aged housewife, Kate Brown, is offered a temporary job as a translator during the summer. Her husband and children are away, and she accepts the work. She makes herself look very smart and revives her sexuality. She goes abroad, has a brief affair with a younger man, and then returns to London. She is ill – part physical, part emotional – and because her house is let, has to stay in a hotel. When she is feeling stronger she rents a room in a young girl's flat and, relieved of all responsibility, and removed from other people's expectations of her, examines her past and present life. During this summer she has a recurrent dream that she is trying to return a seal to the sea, though beset by many obstacles. Finally her dream ends, and Kate returns home to her husband and family.

In this novel Doris Lessing examines female sexuality in more depth than in any of her previous novels. In *Children of Violence* and in *The Golden Notebook* the sexual attitudes of the heroines are intrinsic to the plot, bound up with the narrative. Insights from understanding their sexuality enable both Martha and Anna to know themselves better, and it relates to their actions and motivation. In *The Summer Before the Dark*, however, sexuality is looked at from a wider psychological and also a sociological viewpoint. Using Kate Brown as an example, Mrs Lessing studies the phenomenon of ageing, of becoming physically unattractive (or at least unnoticeable) and makes generalisations about female sexuality which range far beyond this one specific character.

At the beginning of this novel we are introduced to Kate as a conventional, middle-class housewife, neatly dressed, living in a pleasant London suburb. Like the heroine of Mrs Lessing's story, 'To Room Nineteen' (whom she closely resembles), Kate appears to have nothing in the world to worry about. Through the novel her decorous attitudes are juxtaposed with those of her neighbour, Mary Finchley. Mary has no sartorial or sexual inhibitions, and she represents an alternative way of living, instinctual and unrepressed. Married, with three children, she sleeps with whoever she fancies, and feels neither guilt nor shame. Mary, as it were, enacts the suppressed aspects of Kate's personality, and is regarded by her with incomprehension and some envy. Kate realises that Mary is significant to her: 'she was going to have to understand what Mary meant to her, what she was standing for' (p. 91). In contrast to her neighbour's spontaneity, Kate's life seems a network of restricting responsibilities and prohibitions. 'Looking back over nearly a quarter of a century, she saw that that had been the characteristic of her life, passivity, adaptability to others' (p. 21). Her own identity, which has been obliterated by the demands of her husband and children, is painfully reachieved, and *The Summer Before the Dark* is a chronicle of rediscovery.

Kate's earliest awareness of her sexuality was when she spent a year in Lourenço Marques, with her Portuguese grandfather. Beautiful and strictly chaperoned, she becomes conscious of both her sexual power and her social weakness: 'She was flattered by deference to her every wish – but knew that she, the female thing, occupied a carefully defined minor part of her grandfather's life, as his wife had done, and his daughters' (p. 16). Her subsequent life follows this pattern, where she is deferred to superficially, but dominated in reality. After years of domesticity, her presence at an international conference as a translator again exposes her to the heady attentions of men. She realises that it is easy to make herself seem invisible, simply by changing the signals she gives out by her posture.

> For she was conscious . . . as alert to it as if this was the most important fact of her life, that the person who sat there watching, shunned or ignored by men who otherwise would have been attracted to her, was not in the slightest degree different from the person who could bring them all on again towards her by adjusting the picture of herself: lips, a set of facial muscles, eye movements, angle of back and shoulders. (p. 45)

Towards the end of the novel Kate deliberately re-enacts this sexual scenario with workmen on a building site. She walks in front of them wearing her jacket and is not noticed. Then she removes her jacket, revealing her fitted dress, and ties her hair back with a scarf. She walks past seductively, this time to a chorus of wolf-whistles and invitations. She again puts on her jacket, and again walks back unnoticed. She becomes very angry with the realisation that all her life has been a performance to gratify other people: 'This is what you have been doing for years and years and years' (p. 207). With this in mind Mary Finchley's warmhearted amorality becomes not only tolerable but the only sensible way of living. Kate says 'There are times, you know, when . . . I seem to myself like a raving lunatic. Love and duty, and being in love and not being in love, and loving, and behaving well and you should and you shouldn't and you ought and you oughtn't. It's a disease' (p. 216). *The Summer Before the Dark* is a novel full of fury about the ritual manoeuvres of female sexuality. It is as if Mrs Lessing feels that she, through Kate Brown, is newly exposing a great confidence trick, and her vehemence makes one suspect that her observation of her own ageing process is relevant. In an interview with Susan Stamberg she was asked if she was vain about her age, and she replied 'No I don't mind. When I was young I was quite pretty, I'm sorry that's gone, but I don't care all that much . . . the thing is that when you become middle-aged . . . and beyond – you literally become sort of unnoticed. You can just sit and watch and listen, and you don't have to put on any acts.'[33] The tone of this novel is not so much regret at ageing, as at time wasted in false behaviour demanded by conformity to feminine roles.

When Kate returns to London and is ill, her appearance changes dramatically. She loses weight and becomes gaunt. Her hair, once her pride, becomes frizzy and shows a wide band of grey at the roots. She goes to the theatre, and Mrs Lessing describes her perception of the audience in a Swiftian vision which we have already been shown in *The Four-Gated City*: 'animals covered with cloth and bits of fur, ornamented with stones, their faces and claws painted with colour. Everyone had just finished eating animal of some kind' (p. 149). At such moments of heightened awareness Mrs Lessing's characters are often filled with revulsion at their fellow human beings, and Kate is not exempt from this. She feels disgust at her years of vanity which have confined her to a limited range of roles. Her illness, combined with her isolation from her employment and her family, has forced upon her a new persona – or rather, cracked and broken the old one: 'the image had rolled itself up and thrown itself into a corner, leaving behind the face of a sick monkey' (p. 153). It is as if the potential for growth can be set to work only if all the roles sustaining the old personality are wrenched away. No longer mistress, wife, mother, organiser, Kate rents a cheap room to discover who will emerge from this unprecedented vacuum. In Maureen's flat she feels lonely and abandoned. It is 'the first time in her life that she had been alone and outside a cocoon of comfort and protection' (p. 163). She gradually learns not to mother Maureen, and how to live her own life. But a letter from her youngest son, wanting to come home from abroad, snaps Kate back into the housewife and mother roles. Maureen overhears her efficiently organising the rehabilitation of her house, and consequently breaks off her engagement. When Kate asks her why, she says in horror 'I'd do anything, I'd live alone for *always* rather than turn into *that*' (p. 193). '*That*' is the superwoman role Kate excels at, and which she now recognises as a trap. She then cancels all her arrangements, leaving herself free for a few more weeks, because she realises that her work of self-discovery is not yet finished.

Throughout *The Summer Before the Dark* Kate has a serial dream which acts as counterpoint to the realist action. The dream is not incidental but central to the plot; it acts both as a continuing motivating force for the heroine, and as a commentary from her unconscious on her behaviour. Kate dreams that she has found a seal lying stranded on dry rocks in a northern landscape. She begins to carry it downhill to get it to water. It is not necessary for the seal to be defined in terms of precise symbolism. It is helpless and stranded and out of its element, and Kate's discovery and rescue of it parallels her gradual discovery and rescue of her self, lost for twenty-five years. In her second dream Kate becomes more involved with the seal by trying to cure its wounds with herbs, but in her next dream the seal disappears, and is replaced by a turtle. The turtle, having been irradiated after an atom bomb test, walks away from the sea towards its death in a dry hinterland. Kate searches in anguish for her seal, without success. This dream comes at the point in the novel where Kate herself has taken a wrong turning, a bad decision. Instead of pursuing her own quest, however painful, she agrees to go on holiday with a young American. 'She ought to go straight back to England . . . rent a roof for herself . . . and sit quietly and let the cold wind blow as hard as it would. . . . She already knew that Jeffrey Merton . . . when she looked back, would seem to her all dryness and repetition' (p. 67). While she is in Spain with Jeffrey, Kate

dreams that she carries the seal to a house in which she
performs motherly and housewifely duties for her family. She
makes love with a young man, but refuses to stay with him,
telling him that she has to get the seal to the sea. In a later
dream Kate and the seal are threatened by wild animals in an
amphitheatre, and Kate only just has sufficient strength to save
them both. She begins to realise that her survival is bound up
with that of the seal. During her illness, back in England, Kate
dreams that her lover, a king, has danced with her and then
abandoned her for a young girl. She is imprisoned in a pit, and
criticised by her former lover. She knows that the seal is alone
somewhere, believing itself to have been abandoned. This
dream seems to symbolise Kate's youthful marriage, and her
subsequent domestic imprisonment, as well as the more subtle
incarcerations of ageing. The seal, her selfhood, is deserted, but
it is found again in her next dream, near to death. Kate revives
it and continues her journey northwards, towards the sea.

After her illness, Kate dreams less about the seal. But when
she is with Maureen in the flat, she tells her the dream, and it
then returns night after night. It is no longer distinct or
memorable, but leaves her with a feeling of difficulty and
loneliness. Maureen tells Kate that she must not go back to her
family before she has finished her dream. After she is able to
acknowledge the constrictions of love and duty and the 'shoulds'
and 'oughts' in her life, Kate again dreams of the seal. This
time, as she carries the seal towards the sea, she sees a pink
flowering cherry tree in bloom in the snow, and she picks a
twig. She realises that the dream is nearing its end. At last
Kate dreams that the snow has stopped falling, and that the
seal is 'full of life, and, like her, of hope' (p. 227). She sees grass
growing and spring flowers, and looks down onto a sunlit sea:

Her journey was over.
   She saw that the sun was in front of her, not behind, not
far far behind, under the curve of the earth, which was where
it had been for so long. She looked at it, a large, light,
brilliant, buoyant, tumultuous sun that seemed to sing.
(p. 228)

Kate's journey is always northwards with the seal, through
snow and ice. And yet, paradoxically, when she arrives at her

destination, the sea, the snow has melted and the sun is shining. We understand the northward journey to be a metaphor for the pain of self-discovery. The south symbolises warmth and ease, and Kate has to turn her back on easy options. The journey is cold and lonely, and the metaphor used during the novel for Kate's waking life is that of a 'chill wind' blowing through it. Nevertheless, having persisted in carrying the seal to the sea, Kate discovers sun, blue sky and warmth. Her persistence is rewarded, and her self-knowledge is achieved by a letting-go rather than by a process of rational accumulation of knowledge. This brings unexpected light and joy, and after this dream Kate is able to return home.

This novel has been widely criticised for its ending, particularly by feminists. Kate's decision to return home is seen as a defeat, a denial of what she has become at the end of her psychic pilgrimage. But surely this is to miss the point. Kate has changed in the course of the novel. She has allowed her household to function without her. She has grown out of the nannying role, whether in relation to her own children, or to the delegates of Global International. It is unimaginable that she will revert to the person she was at the beginning of the summer. Having restored her scarred and wounded self from aridity into its element, she can begin anew anywhere she chooses, even in her old environment.

The Memoirs of a Survivor is a novel which sums up what has happened to Mrs Lessing's fictive concerns since she wrote *The Golden Notebook*. The futility of investment in personal relationships, the growing attention to 'inner space' and the human potential for spiritual growth, the consequent alienation from the material world; these themes have been latent in Mrs Lessing's fiction from the beginning. In *The Golden Notebook* she began to deal with them explicitly, a process continued in *Landlocked* and *The Four-Gated City*. They are crucial themes in her next two novels, and in *The Memoirs of a Survivor* she makes them central. But the difference is that the sense of struggle is absent. Anna, Martha, Charles Watkins and Kate Brown are all fighting for their spiritual lives: the first person narrator in this novel, however, has a calm tone of – not resignation, exactly – but clear-sighted acceptance of what is happening in both her inner and outer worlds. The very calmness with which

the narrator describes disintegration and chaos is itself
horrifying, and Mrs Lessing skilfully uses this discrepancy to
shock her readers.

For the first time in Doris Lessing's work, realism and
symbolism mesh totally. In her earlier novels dreams and
madness were the vehicles for the exploration of spiritual or
psychic states. For example, Martha's and Linda's 'madness' is
described realistically, as is Charles Watkins's, but the state of
so-called madness allows the narrator to write about symbolic
events and evolutions of the mind. In *The Memoirs of a Survivor*,
however, Mrs Lessing makes it clear from the start that the text
is both literal and symbolic in that the narrator is first able to
look through, then to *go* through the solid wall of her flat, into
another place. Realism is thus jettisoned very early in the
novel. The wall becomes the division between the conscious
and unconscious minds of the narrator, and the rooms and
gardens beyond it are areas of the unconscious which she
explores. Doris Lessing does this very easily; the transition from
the realistic to the symbolic is achieved without signs of strain
or undue anxiety about convincing the reader. It is as if Mrs
Lessing has by this time become so used to moving between the
outer and inner worlds in her own life, that her fiction reflects
the ease of it.

The novel is set in a city where most services have ceased
and where anarchy prevails. Commodities and food are in short
supply. The unnamed woman narrator lives in a flat and is
thinking about leaving the increasingly beleaguered city. One
day a child of about 12 is left for her to look after. The child,
Emily, has a pet with her, a strange dog–cat called Hugo. The
novel describes their life together over a period of about three
years. Emily becomes involved with the leader of a gang of
children, and for her a lifetime of experience is compressed,
encapsulated into a few years. By the age of 15 she is a mature,
wise woman. Mrs Lessing accelerates her maturity partly as a
realistic sign of the times which cannot accommodate a normally
prolonged childhood, partly as a technique through which Emily
represents the narrator's own life in retrospect, so that Emily
and the narrator are one person. While looking after the girl
and watching her grow up, the narrator explores the rooms
behind the wall. She sees scenes from Emily's childhood, which
are also scenes from her own childhood. She goes over them in

detail, reworking the experiences, understanding them and the effect they have had on her subsequent life. Finally, the realism of the novel collapses completely, and the narrator, accompanied by Emily, her lover Gerald and a group of children they have looked after, and the dog–cat Hugo, all walk through the wall 'into another order of world altogether' (p. 190).

Mrs Lessing describes this novel as 'an attempt at autobiography'.[34] Although it is not literally an autobiography in the accepted sense, it is perhaps far closer to one than many critics have allowed. In it, Doris Lessing deals with aspects of her childhood which are so conspicuously omitted in *Martha Quest*, where the novel begins with the heroine as an adolescent. In interviews, Mrs Lessing has hinted at the difficult relationship she had with her mother, and in *Children of Violence* the character of Mrs Quest indicates the areas of conflict that may have arisen in real life. In *The Four-Gated City* the intended visit of her mother gives Martha a nervous breakdown, as if it revived all the issues she had not been able to face up to, and had avoided by coming to England. Of course, much of this material must remain speculative in relation to the real lives of Doris Lessing and her mother. Nevertheless, all that can be said is that it feels true, it has the veracity of fiction dealing imaginatively with real and painful issues. It would seem that Doris Lessing had not fully explored this relationship until she wrote *The Memoirs of a Survivor* and indeed, this novel does give the impression of being an exorcism, leading to reconciliation and peace. By reliving the most painful of her early memories, the narrator is able to see that her mother also inherited a legacy of bad parenting, and perhaps inevitably passed it on.

At the beginning of this novel Mrs Lessing makes clear the importance to the narrator of the inner life: 'I was feeling as if the centre of gravity of my life had moved, balances had shifted somewhere, and I was beginning to believe – uncomfortably, still – that what went on behind the wall might be every bit as important as my ordinary life in that neat and comfortable, if shabby, flat' (p. 14). On an early visit beyond the wall the narrator glimpses the shadow of a face, welcoming, reassuring, which she feels must be exiled from that place, which is dirty and uncared for. On subsequent visits through the wall the experiences are either 'personal' or 'impersonal'. The personal scenes re-enact episodes from the narrator's (and Emily's)

childhood, and the impersonal ones offer a task to be done –
usually of cleaning or painting the rooms, tasks reminiscent of
Charles Watkins's cleaning of the circle in the city square to
receive the crystal disc. Mrs Lessing seems to suggest that the
unconscious mind has been neglected, and needs scrupulous
attention. From the 'personal' scenes there is a sense of
constriction, of no alternatives; from the impersonal a sense of
freedom and possibilities. We are shown scenes of Emily as a
tiny baby, screaming with hunger because she is fed only at
strictly regulated intervals. We are shown a little girl of 4,
whose baby brother gets far more attention than she does.
Later on, the girl of 5 or 6 feels guilty for existing. She listens to
a nagging monologue from her mother to a neighbour about
how exhausted she is made by the children. In this novel Doris
Lessing captures with great psychological accuracy the inescapable effect of early parental influences, long forgotten by
the conscious memory:

> The hard, accusing voice went on and on, would always go
> on, had always gone on, nothing could stop it, could stop
> these emotions, this pain, this guilt at having been born at
> all, born to cause such pain and annoyance and difficulty.
> The voice would nag on there for ever, could never be turned
> off, and even when the sound was turned low in memory,
> there must be a permanent pressure of dislike, resentment.
> (p. 65)

In subsequent scenes the narrator/Emily child endures the
cruel tickling of her father, rife with sexual ambivalence,
disguised as fun. She longs for safe, warm, physical contact
with her mother, but is denied the cuddles she asks for. She
endures the fact that her younger brother is the favourite, and
that she is considered a nuisance. In one scene Emily has
defecated in her bed, and is given a rigorous scrubbing in an
overhot bath, to the repetitive accompaniment of her mother's
anger: 'Emily, you are dirty, *naughty*, oh *disgusting*, you are a
filthy, dirty dirty girl, Emily' (p. 130). Her sobbing echoes for
days throughout the narrator's flat, but when she tries to locate
the crying child she encounters not Emily, but Emily's mother,
who herself is weeping: 'the little arms, desperate for comfort
. . . would one day be those great arms that had never been

taught tenderness' (p. 134). And, of course, were not able to give tenderness in turn to the small child who is at the centre of this novel.

Emily's final manifestation in the narrator's visionary flashbacks is as a girl dressed provocatively in a tight red dress, parading a grotesque, doll-like sexuality. She confronts her mother defiantly, and gradually grows smaller and smaller, and vanishes in a puff of red smoke. It is as if the emergence of adolescent sexuality becomes distorted in her mother's eyes, and the final breaking of the tenuous, hostile relationship is the inevitable outcome of her unloving childhood. In these personal visions of the narrator, Doris Lessing has courageously examined the unwritten material that lies behind *Martha Quest*. Indeed, one could go as far as to say that the spectre of that small, unloved child is the motivating force behind all her work up to this point. In her non-fiction book *In Pursuit of the English* she says 'I chase love and fame all the time' (p. 10), and in her prolific output there is an undertone of irremediable loneliness.

While Emily is forming relationships, taking a lover, accepting responsibilities – in short, growing up – the narrator is examining the impersonal visions through the wall. These visions, unlike the personal scenes of childhood, represent the future potential of the narrator's self. The metaphor of the wall as a barrier to enlightenment recurs in Sufi writings and is used by R. D. Laing. In *The Politics of Experience* he writes what is, in effect, a summary of the themes of Doris Lessing's later fiction:

The fountain has not played itself out, the flame still shines, the river still flows, the spring still bubbles forth, the light has not faded. But between *us* and It there is a veil which is more like fifty feet of solid concrete. *Deus absconditus.* Or we have absconded. Already everything in our time is directed to categorizing and segregating this reality from objective facts. This is precisely the concrete wall. Intellectually, emotionally, inter-personally, organizationally, intuitively, theoretically, we have to blast our way through the solid wall, even if at the risk of chaos, madness and death. For from *this* side of the wall, this is the risk. There are no assurances, no guarantees. (Ch. 6)

And in *The Four-Gated City* Linda says 'if you go on always, testing the walls for weakness, for a thin place, one day, you will simply step outside, free' (Pt. 4, Ch. 2). In *The Memoirs of a Survivor* the rooms through the wall are beautiful, but in great disarray, and the narrator sets about cleaning them. It is a thankless procedure, however, because whenever she re-enters the rooms they are again in disorder, and she has to do the cleaning all over again. The process is analogous to learning at a spiritual level: it is not a straightforward, linear advancement, but a series of understandings, forgettings, and relearning. At the heart of this novel is an image which is central to our understanding of it: the narrator finds a hexagonal-shaped room with a carpet spread on the floor. The carpet has a design with no colours, and the people in the room are engaged in fitting fragments of material on to the carpet which bring light and colour to it. This metaphor links with an earlier one in *The Golden Notebook* where Anna talks with her Jungian therapist about a similar process:

> You talk about individuation. So far what it has meant to me is this: that the individual recognises one part after another of his earlier life as an aspect of the general human experience. When he can say: What I did then, what I felt then, is only the reflection of that great archetypal dream, or epic story, or stage in history, then he is free, because he has separated himself from the experience, or fitted it like a piece of mosaic into a very old pattern, and by the act of setting it into place, is free of the individual pain of it. (p. 458)

Aspects of each person's experience are understood by seeing how they fit into an overall design. In *The Memoirs of a Survivor* Mrs Lessing is saying that there is such a design, if only we could see it. The seeing of it, she implies, involves an exploration of our unconscious minds, and an acceptance that it is necessary to work at a psychic level to make up for neglecting this aspect of our personality.

A curious creature in this novel is Hugo, the dog–cat hybrid that Emily brings with her to the flat, and who remains loyal to her despite her involvement with the gang-leader Gerald, and her long absences from the flat. Hugo is always in danger, since dogs and cats are eaten during this period of anarchy and scarce food supplies. The narrator realises that Hugo's function is to look after Emily, but it is not clear what he symbolises. Perhaps a clue is that 'Hugo' means 'mind', and it is significant that whenever Emily is with her lover she leaves Hugo behind. He cannot be accommodated in the gang (which threatens to kill them) or in Emily's romantic life, which, as the narrator shows, leaves no room for growth or maturing of the mind or spirit. At the end of the novel, Hugo is ready to go through the wall, 'looking into it as if at last what he wanted and needed and knew would happen was here, and he was ready for it' (p. 189).

Throughout *The Memoirs of a Survivor* the narrator makes clear that part of what she has survived are the strictures laid down by society for the behaviour of women, and the disease of romantic love. She watches Emily confront these forces, as if regarding her own life in retrospect. When Emily and Gerald try to run a commune, they are horrified that they find it necessary to establish a hierarchy for its efficient functioning. The narrator tells her that the pressures of society are such that 'Everybody has to be taught to find a place in a structure . . . to obey' (p. 117). She goes on to say: 'It starts when you are born. . . . She's a good girl. She's a bad girl. Have you been a good girl today? I hear you've been a bad girl. . . . It's all false, it's got to do with nothing real. . . . "Do as I tell you and I'll tell you you are good." It's a trap and we're all in it' (p. 118). When Gerald deserts Emily for another girl, she feels all the pain of rejection. The narrator understands only too well what Emily is feeling.

> Her eyes met mine. They were the eyes of a mature woman of thirty-five or forty . . . she would never willingly suffer any of it again. . . . She knew 'falling in love' was an illness to be endured, a trap which might lead her to betray her own nature, her good sense and her real purposes. It was not a door to anything but itself: not a key to living. (p. 176)

This does not come across to the reader as cynicism or even pessimism. Rather, it reminds me of someone who, having completed a long and arduous journey across difficult terrain, is pointing out the pitfalls to a future traveller: that path looks inviting but leads nowhere; pain and loneliness are inevitable and must be endured. Mrs Lessing's tone is one of tired but calm acceptance, in contrast to the fighting exasperation of some of her earlier novels. There is no rhetoric of persuasion. Take it or leave it, she seems to say, but this is how it is.

The reader is not left with a sense of frustration, however, because in this novel the confines of 'how it is' in this world are finally transcended. Not only that: Mrs Lessing acknowledges a similar potential latent in everybody, however hidden or unrealised it may be. Emily makes a friend of June, the daughter of an indigent, feckless, happy-go-lucky family called the Ryans. 'The Ryans' epitomise what was unassimilable in the society that is now disintegrating, and the narrator even has a technical difficulty in knowing where to place them in the narration, since they represent what cannot be easily incorporated into a coherent system. The family are impoverished and filthy; they live for the moment and have no savings, make no plans. With some irony, the narrator shows how their life-style is actually more appropriate to the times described in the novel than the careful respectability of increasingly redundant middle-class values. Yet June feels so valueless that she leaves Emily, her friend, without even saying goodbye. It is only the narrator, nurturing her own awareness of the spiritual wealth available to everyone, who allows June her true value: she

> thought of what riches there were in store for these creatures and all the others like them; and though it was hard to maintain a knowledge of that other world with its scent and running waters and its many plants while I sat here in this dull shabby daytime room, the pavement outside seething as usual with its trival life – I did hold it. I kept it in my mind. I was able to do this. (p. 143)

Finally, when the wall opens to allow the characters access to the world beyond it, the narrator again glimpses the numinous presence – goddess, Muse, Earth Mother – she saw briefly at the beginning of the novel. Hugo and Emily 'both walked quickly behind that One who went ahead showing them the way out of this collapsed little world into another order of world altogether' (p. 190). The walls dissolve, the division between the inner and outer worlds finally disappears, and unity is achieved. Thus the novel ends on a note of affirmation, which is not just the culmination of this novel, but of all Mrs

Lessing's work so far. Martha's 'quest' ends here. Communism, feminism, all the 'causes' espoused throughout Mrs Lessing's canon, have been shown to offer incomplete solutions. And since these causes have failed, Mrs Lessing indicates that the only possible path to survival is gnostic. *The Memoirs of a Survivor* is a very practical book about recognising, acknowledging and working with the transcendent possibilities of the unconscious mind. For its author this working is a method of achieving the coherence towards which all her energies as a writer and a woman have been directed.

6

Canopus in Argos: Archives

After the publication of *The Memoirs of a Survivor* one critic wrote: 'One wonders where Lessing can go from here.'[35] And indeed, the tone of transcendence at the end of that novel is such that it is not surprising that Mrs Lessing moves out of this world altogether for her next five novels – a series which takes a cosmic viewpoint and which has the overall title *Canopus in Argus: Archives*. In her preface to *Shikasta*, the first in the series, she defends science fiction and science fiction writers:

> These dazzlers have mapped our world, or worlds, for us, have told us what is going on and in ways no one else has done, have described our nasty present long ago, when it was still the future and the official scientific spokesmen were saying that all manner of things now happening were impossible – who have played the indispensable and (at least at the start) thankless role of the despised illegitimate son who can afford to tell truths the respectable siblings either do not dare, or, more likely, do not notice because of their respectability.

It is a new phenomenon for a 'respectable' novelist to turn to space fiction, and some Lessing critics have experienced difficulty with this change of direction in her work. It demands a fresh perspective, a long view. Instead of focusing on one person in a small town, or on several people in one country, Mrs Lessing's imagination takes off into space and she is exhilarated by the freedom. 'It was clear I had made – or found – a new world for myself, a realm where the petty fates of planets, let alone individuals, are only aspects of cosmic evolution expressed in the rivalries and interactions of great galactic Empires' (preface to *Shikasta*). And the cool, detached tone of the archivist suits the perspective. In *Shikasta* the narrator is appropriately distanced from his material in a way unprecedented in Mrs Lessing's work. Her previous narrators' involvement in her plots has entailed emotional and psychological involvement also. In *Shikasta* there is pain and difficulty for the narrator, but it is understood in the context of a cosmic scheme, and therefore the personal signifies little.

Shikasta chronicles the decline of the planet earth, which is part of a galaxy influenced by a benign planet, Canopus; a technological planet, Sirius, and an evil planet, Shammat. Canopus has colonised Shikasta (which means 'broken' in Persian)[36] and in this account we are shown the pathology of its disintegration. Shikasta was formerly peopled with superior beings who lived to a great age in harmony with each other, and who had telepathic powers. As the benevolent link between Shikasta and Canopus weakens, Shikasta suffers from increasing individualism, leading to wars and destruction. Agents from Canopus attempt to remind the degenerate population of their past, and of their latent potential. Like Charles Watkins in *Briefing for a Descent into Hell*, certain people are reincarnated for this purpose, and, like Sufi mystics, they take on the protective guise of the culture they are placed in. In addition, a character from *The Four-Gated City*, Lynda Coldridge, re-emerges in this novel as a woman with extra-sensory perception, a faculty necessary for humanity's survival. Finally, *Shikasta* covers the same ground as *The Four-Gated City*: destruction of much of the planet, and the gradual, tentative beginning again.

The form of this novel is appropriate to Mrs Lessing's rejection of the personal (and to her eyes, limited) point of view. The narration is partly in the first person, but the narrator varies. Sometimes it is the Canopean agent, Johor, at other times other agents and envoys. Sometimes it is Lynda Coldridge, or a girl called Rachel Sherban. The tone of the narration is also varied. Official reports in bureaucratic language, or formal extracts from the History of Shikasta contrast with informal letters and with the intimacy of Rachel Sherban's journal. The characterisation is fleeting. The closest the novel comes to a realist delineation of character is in the attention given to the reincarnation of Johor, George Sherban. The settings change frequently: galaxies, planets, hemispheres, countries, cities. There is no loving construction of one particular place, such as the Rhodesian bush in the African stories and novels. Families and agents move around, and during the last days of Shikasta individual countries are ruled by international committees.

The time-span of this novel is in millennia rather than decades or centuries, and for a reader accustomed to a traditional novel this takes some getting used to. At one point Johor says 'It is thirty thousand years since I was in Shikasta; 31,505 to be exact' (p. 135), and 'an ice age is nothing, it is a few thousand years – the ice comes, and then it goes' (p. 251). This temporal dislocation helps the reader to understand the scale of Mrs Lessing's vision. It is as if she is determined that we should think in cosmic, rather than individual or national, or even merely human terms, and some of the difficulty of this novel lies in coming to terms with this gigantic canvas. The personal, the local, the chronological are all subsumed by an authorial attitude which makes them not only anachronistic, but also irrelevant by its urgency.

Early in the novel Mrs Lessing makes clear the nature of Shikasta's affliction: 'To identify with ourselves as individuals – this is the very essence of the Degenerative Disease, and everyone of us in the Canopean Empire is taught to value ourselves only insofar as we are in harmony with the plan, the phases of our evolution' (p. 55). Johor explains that what has kept Shikasta in harmony until now is a fine current from Canopus, called 'SOWF – the substance-of-we-feeling'. This sense of unity with the cosmos, a feeling of mutual harmony, is the central aspiration in Mrs Lessing's later novels. But in *Canopus in Argos: Archives* this seems to be contradicted by the colonial policy of the Canopeans. On one hand, interdependence and mutualism are extolled; on the other it is made clear that Shikasta's health depends on its allegiance and obedience to its colonial overlord. The crucial difficulty for the reader is in accepting the idea of colonialism as genuinely benign and, even if benign, as an appropriate relationship. As Lorna Sage points out:

The most striking legacy, in *Canopus*, is the structuring assumption that different groups inevitably overlap and interfere with each other, so that – to put it crudely – it is not a matter of oppression *or* co-existence but of 'good' colonisers or 'bad' colonisers. The Canopeans (the good) are the group of groups, always at work to turn wars of words into silent symbiosis, and so on, agents of a (mostly) invisible Empire. And they are – despite their modest disguises – figures of authority, unmistakeably. Residual authority, perhaps, but all the more absolute for that.[37]

When Johor orders the Giants to leave Shikasta, some of them refuse. 'I said to them that those who decided to stay would be committing Disobedience. For the first time in their history they would not be in conformity with Canopean Law. . . . I said that disobedience to the Master Plan was always, everywhere, the first sign of the Degenerative Disease' (p. 65). The archival tone of the text to some extent disguises Mrs Lessing's moral bias, but she is certainly of the opinion that the inhabitants of Shikasta (which is Earth) have made a poor job of running the planet, and her anger shows through in the trial scene at the end. Nevertheless, one is uneasy at her alternative of 'obedience to the Master Plan'.

It is their detachment from human emotions which characterises the agents from Mrs Lessing's other worlds. Charles Watkins in *Briefing for a Descent into Hell* and George Sherban in *Shikasta* (both agents from other worlds) are unemotional and self-contained. Consequently they both greatly distress the women in their lives, who want more commitment than the men are able to offer. In *Shikasta* Rachel Sherban points out to her brother than Suzannah loves him, and does not see their relationship in quite such a clinical light as he does. Unlike Charles Watkins in a similar situation, George becomes embarrassed, something Rachel has never seen before. The transitory and misguided nature of human love is a frequent theme in Mrs Lessing's later work, and in *Shikasta* Lynda expresses her feelings of emotional claustrophobia which have already been shown in *The Four-Gated City*. 'Why do people have to get into one place and live together? Lick. Lick. People who are like each other are together anyway. That is what I think. They don't have to go lick lick' (p. 236). Lynda has of course been classified as 'mad' and the cool flatness of her tone is easily labelled as 'insane'. But Doris Lessing makes it clear that she is on the side of Lynda's perceptions, which have been ratified earlier in *The Four-Gated City* as well as in this novel.

The degeneration of Shikasta becomes such that truth-tellers are not believed, and those people with paranormal capacities such as Lynda are locked in mental hospitals. A Shammat agent sends a report back to his planet on the fate of four national leaders who try to warn the inhabitants of Shikasta that conditions on the planet are worse than they have been led to believe. When all four are deposed or killed, the Shammat agent triumphantly concludes his report: 'These tests have proved that the planet is immune to truth' (p. 326). A huge mock trial is held to examine the causes of the planet's degeneration, and the indictment is as follows:

> That it is the white races of this world that have destroyed it, corrupted it, made possible the wars that have ruined it, have laid the basis for the war that we all fear, have poisoned the seas, and the waters, and the air, have stolen everything for themselves, have laid waste the goodness of the earth from the North to the South, and from East to West, have behaved always with arrogance, and contempt, and barbarity towards others, and have been above all guilty of the supreme crime of stupidity – and must now accept the burden of culpability, as murderers, thieves, and destroyers, for the dreadful situation we now all find ourselves in. (p. 388)

In the testimonies following Mrs Lessing presents damning evidence of the white man's disastrous colonial policies in North and South America, and in Africa. The representative white man on trial, a Canopean reincarnation called John Brent-Oxford, while not exonerating the whites, draws attention to the exploitation of each other by black and coloured peoples. By the end of the trial, and of the novel, the evidence against the possible (let alone desirable) continuation of the species is so strong, that one feels the subsequent destruction is not only inevitable, but deserved. As in *The Four-Gated City*, there are survivors from the disaster, who make a tentative new beginning. In a final lyrical section the inheritors of a new order look back at the past with pity. 'Poor people of the past, poor poor people, so many of them, for long thousands of years, not knowing anything, fumbling and stumbling and longing for something different but not knowing what had happened to them or what they longed for' (p. 447).

Shikasta is an awkward novel to read, partly because of the wide range of viewpoints, styles and time-shifts. Mrs Lessing has said of it '*Shikasta* is a mess, but at any rate it is a new mess.'[38] A prevailing factor is the distant, archivist's perspective, but sometimes Mrs Lessing is hoisted by the petard of her own insistence on this distant overview; for example, it makes her sudden close focus on the Rhodesian government of Ian Smith seem absurdly parochial. Nevertheless, the variety of focus is contained in an impeccably stable framework. Doris Lessing has worked out her galactic empire in meticulous, almost irritating detail, and the inconsistencies that appear are not usually technical, but as was said earlier, ideological. Her emphasis in her novels up to this point has been on a personal enlightenment, and her tone, although increasingly detached, has been that of a benign (if gently pessimistic) teacher. In *Shikasta* this changes, and there is a note of condescension running throughout the novel. She views the planet Earth from a great height, as it were, as if she were not still part of the human race she so despises. It is a relief that the next novel of *Canopus in Argos: Archives* does not continue this trend, but is different both in tone and in orientation.

The Marriages Between Zones Three, Four, and Five began in Doris Lessing's mind twenty years or so before it came out as a novel. She says of it:

> It was written out of this experience. When I was in my late thirties and early forties my love life was in a state of chaos and disarray and generally no good to me or anybody else and I was, in fact, and I knew it, in a pretty bad way. Unconsciously I used a certain therapeutic technique which just emerged from my unconscious. What I did was I had a kind of imaginary landscape . . . in which I had a male and a female figure in various relationships. . . . I made the man a man who was very strong as a man, responsible for what he had to do and autonomous in himself and I made the woman the same because I was very broken down in various ways at that time, and this went on for some years in fact. And then I read about it; it is a Jungian technique. They tell you that if you have some area in yourself which you can't cope with, to do this; you take some part of you which is weak and

deliberately fantasize it strong. . . . So this book has come out of years of the closest possible work of the imagination.[39]

The re-emergence of this work in this form is interesting as an example of what the unconscious mind can do, left with promising material. Mrs Lessing wrote this novel very quickly and easily, because the 'work' had been done before hand. The novel reflects this ease. It has a lyricism, a coherence and an assurance of tone, almost as if Mrs Lessing were taking a holiday from dealing with the cosmic difficulties outlined in *Shikasta*, and to which she returns in *The Sirian Experiments*.

Al·Ith is queen of Zone Three, a gentle, sensitive country where telepathy is practised both by inhabitants and by their animals. She is ordered to marry Ben Ata, king of Zone Four, a primitive country by comparison, where war and aggression are the predominant activities. Zone Five is an even wilder region, and the enemy of both Zones Three and Four. Throughout the novel Al·Ith looks up to the blue, rarified atmosphere of Zone Two, which is advanced and enlightened. After a great deal of disagreement and quarrelling, Al·Ith and Ben Ata come to love each other, and Al·Ith gives birth to his son, Arusi. She is told to leave Zone Four, and Ben Ata is ordered to marry Vahshi, the queen of Zone Five. Al·Ith returns to Zone Three, not as a queen, but to work as a peasant. She spends more and more time looking up at Zone Two, and eventually goes there, never to return. The cultures of the Zones mingle, so that the arranged marriages have an enlightening and beneficial effect on each area, formerly self-contained and unreceptive.

The novel is an allegorical treatment of the material that was used in *The Golden Notebook*, and in this new form Mrs Lessing draws attention to its stylised quality. The chronicler or narrator comes from Zone Three, and describes the events with an awareness of writing down the history of which legends are made. Every so often a set-piece is described, such as Al·Ith arguing with the Zone Four soldiers, or Al·Ith and Ben Ata inspecting his army. The chronicler reminds the reader that such schemes have been depicted by artists who may have added some detail, or changed some aspect, and that they have passed into the mythology of Zone Three. Thus the narration of *The Marriages Between Zones Three, Four, and Five* describes events in terms both of realism and of iconology, and this process is distancing. The reader is involved in what happens, and then asked to stand back, as it were, and look at the scenes as rendered into art: formal, distorted from reality, and imbued with symbolism merely by the fact of their selection for a permanent record. Thus, the exchange between Al·Ith and Ben Ata's soldiers sent to accompany her to Zone Four becomes a scene enlivened by small creatures – birds, deer – and entitled 'Al·Ith's animals'. The chronicler goes on to say: 'I take the liberty of doubting whether the actual occasion impressed itself so dramatically on the soldiers, or even on Al·Ith' (p. 19). Art falsifies, it is implied, and by drawing our attention to the fictionality of the paintings we are encouraged by the chronicler to believe in the written narrative, which gains veracity by comparison.

I said earlier that the material of this novel, the advantages and difficulties of cultural miscegenation, is that of *The Golden Notebook*, but the plot is similar to that of *The Memoirs of a Survivor*, and is to do with the process of transcendence. Al·Ith is ordered to mate with an alien king, and to his country she brings the ideas and aspirations of Zone Three. From Zone Four she looks up at the beautiful snow-covered mountains of her former kingdom although this practice is forbidden to the subjects of Ben Ata. When she returns to Zone Three for a visit, Al·Ith gazes up into the blueness of Zone Two, and is aware of some deep knowledge inside herself, related to this region. 'It's there . . . if only I could grasp it' (p. 77). In this novel the zones seem to correspond to stages of enlightenment. Zone Five is the most primitive, and Zone One, which is scarcely mentioned, is presumably the highest state. Zone Two corresponds with the world behind the wall in *The Memoirs of a Survivor*, and Mrs Lessing uses it as another metaphor to describe the enlightened mind and new ways of seeing. We are told that Al·Ith was aware of Zone Two as a child, and when she and her sister Murti gaze at Zone Two from the top of their palace, Murti turns to her and says 'Why did we forget it?' In Zone Three references to Zone Two are made in children's singing games, but have been forgotten by the adults. In Zone Four the women, in a secret ritual, dance and sing and finally break their country's law by gazing longingly at the mountains of Zone Three. A deep, long-forgotten knowledge is manifested in scraps of old rhymes, a sweet, high song, stirrings of recognition. These fleeting, elusive references recur in Mrs Lessing's work from *Landlocked* onwards, and her consistent reworking of this theme has to do with the difficulty of using rational, linear language to describe it.

Throughout this novel Mrs Lessing emphasises that the spiritual legacy is held in trust, albeit tentatively and often very faintly, by the women and children. Zone Three is a zone of feeling and intuition (traditionally 'feminine' attributes), and is an apparently Utopian society without violence or destruction or oppression. Men can be either 'biological' or 'mind' fathers, and share in the care and nurturing of their children. The zone is one of harmony and beauty and peace. Zone Four is a place of fighting and brutality, and its values are aggressively 'masculine'. Women are raped and kept submissive. Young boys join a children's army at an early age. Any spiritual aspirations are held by the women, and in secret. Mrs Lessing shows the gradual effect of Al·Ith on Ben Ata and Zone Four. Al·Ith teaches him how to make love with sensitivity and wit, and changes many of his stereotyped ideas about female and male roles. It might seem that Mrs Lessing's bias is towards Zone Three, but in fact at the beginning of the novel she shows that the Zone is becoming sterile. The birth-rate is falling and even the animals are not conceiving. Al·Ith's abrasive experience of Zone Four is necessary to shake her complacency about her own country, and to revitalise it. Moreover, it is not simply Zone Four's animal qualities that are needed to energise Al·Ith and Zone Three. While it is beautiful and harmonious and full of feeling, it has forgotten a higher and more spiritual dimension. Mrs Lessing seems almost to be gently satirising those people in the world who aspire to create Utopias which, however beautiful, may still not take proper account of mankind's spiritual needs. Even a Utopia like Zone Three is fruitless without access to a higher zone of spirituality. Paradoxically, it is only when Al·Ith visits the more earthy, primitive Zone Four that she sees as if for the first time the high mountains of her own country. While in Zone Four, however, she becomes infected with some of its maladies. After the birth of her child she becomes dull and ugly. Her love-making changes, and for the first time in her life she experiences the feeling of jealousy. Yet, Mrs Lessing implies, this descent into a lower state is necessary for Al·Ith to begin to yearn for the potentialities of

Zone Two. It is almost as if the psychological climate of Zone Three was too harmonious, too happily autonomous to stimulate a desire for any other kind of existence.

When Ben Ata is finely attuned to Al·Ith he is ordered (presumably by the remote, controlling Canopeans) to marry Vahshi, the queen of Zone Five. Vahshi is wild and primitive, and in comparison Ben Ata now seems sensitive and civilised. Her country is one of sensation and spontaneity, and Ben Ata admires her soldiers' methods of fighting. Ben Ata teaches Vahshi to think, and to stop plundering the weaker tribes of her country. Consequently, instead of fighting between Zones Four and Five there is increased communication. Ben Ata's experience of Zone Five changes him in ways similar to Al·Ith's experiences of Zone Four. When he returns home after his time with Vahshi he teaches his son Arusi to look up to the mountains, and this practice is no longer discouraged among his people. Gradually the values of the different zones permeate each other, and the novel ends on a lyrical and moving note from the narrator, the chronicler of Zone Three.

> There was a continuous movement now, from Zone Five and to Zone Four. And from Zone Four to Zone Three – and from us, up the pass. There was a lightness, a freshness, and an enquiry and a remarking and an inspiration where there had been only stagnation. And closed frontiers. . . . The movement is not all one way – not by any means . . . our songs and tales are told and sung in the sandy camps and around the desert fires of Zone Five. (p. 299)

The reader is left with the sense of infinite possibilities. Zone Five is dealt with in a fairly perfunctory way, as if merely to exemplify the continuation of the chain of response begun in this novel. One has the feeling that Vahshi will soon be ordered to marry the king of Zone Six, and so the process will go on.

So: a love story? Another way of looking at Anna and Saul? A metaphor about the integration of the personality? An allegory of the necessity and the process of spiritual growth? *The Marriages Between Zones Three, Four and Five* is all these things, and it is a good example of how Mrs Lessing combines realism with the fantastic, the symbolic and the archetypal. The novel sounds and resounds on several levels, but the final achievement

is remarkably flowing and harmonious. It is a close-up of part
of the Canopean cosmos, and the chronicler's single narrative
perspective is welcome after the shifting viewpoints and tones
in *Shikasta*. But from this comparatively small and intimate
world of the Zones, Mrs Lessing returns to the vast canvas of
her cosmic empire with *The Sirian Experiments*.

In an 'afterword' to the fourth volume of *Canopus in Argos:
Archives*, Doris Lessing says that the third volume, *The Sirian
Experiments*, 'came to be written as a direct result of nearly fifty
years of being fascinated by the two British expeditions to the
Antarctic led by Robert Falcon Scott; the first in 1901–4, and
the second in 1910–13.' She goes on to say 'No, it was not snow
and ice as such, but rather some social processes, of that time
and this, so strongly illuminated by the expeditions, that
interest me' (*The Making of the Representative for Planet 8*, p. 162).
Mrs Lessing is clearly intrigued by the shift in national
prejudices and assumptions, which were then exemplified by
concepts such as 'duty', 'heroism' and 'patriotism', and which
now seem at best absurd, at worst pernicious, but certainly
anachronistic. She is also interested in the Scott expeditions as
examples of a quest for transcendence: 'This need to break out
of our ordinary possibilities . . . may well be the deepest one we
have' (pp. 176–7). Mrs Lessing shows that the 'divine discontent'
felt by Scott and by Edward Wilson in particular, is analogous
to that felt by Ambien II, the narrator of *The Sirian Experiments*.
Ambien II is aware of the limitations of an advanced
technological society, and the novel focuses on the processes
of change which may succeed such an awareness. Scott's
expeditions, although overtly for the purposes of scientific
exploration, actually elevate empiricism to a level of high
spirituality. 'We travelled for Science' says Cherry-Garrard,[40] as
if for the Holy Grail, and the language of his account is mystical
rather than scientific in tone.

Mrs Lessing says: 'I think there must be definite lifespans for
ideas or sets of related ideas. They are born (or reborn), come
to maturity, decay, die, are replaced. If we do not at least ask
ourselves if this is in fact a process, if we do not make the
attempt to treat the mechanisms of ideas as something we may
study with impartiality, what hope have we of controlling them?'
(p. 170). *The Sirian Experiments* is an attempt to look at the ebb

and flow of ideas, an examination through allegory of what
influences or causes deep changes in our ways of thinking.

In it, Mrs Lessing returns to her cosmic empire of Canopus,
Sirius and Shammat, and she looks at the conflicting values of
Sirius and Canopus as enacted through their respective colonial
policies on Shikasta, known to Sirius as Rohanda. The narrator,
one of the rulers of Sirius, is a dry, cool, bureaucratic woman,
not easily swayed. Like the chronicler of *The Marriages Between
Zones Three, Four, and Five* she offers her account of events as a
're-interpretation of history, from a certain point of view. An
unpopular point of view, even now: until recently, impossible'
(p. 20). Through her narrators in *Shikasta*, *Marriages* and *The
Sirian Experiments* Mrs Lessing herself is also recounting human
history, offering different perspectives on why we are now at
such a potentially disastrous stage of our development. She
teases at this theme, returning to it from various angles to try to
shed light on it. Her interest in trying to diagnose the mechanics
of change is linked to her awareness of the danger we are in by
continuing on the same course. It is really necessary to read *The
Sirian Experiments* (as indeed all the *Canopus in Argos: Archives*)
with a consciousness of their relevance to ourselves, and not
simply as a fable unrelated to our contemporary predicament.

From Ambien II we learn that although the technological
development of Sirius is extremely advanced, the Sirians suffer
from severe anxiety about the purpose of their lives: 'existential
problem melancholia' (p. 99). Their technology, creating endless
leisure, does not solve their problems. On the contrary, its very
sophistication creates new ones. For example, a series of
carefully carried out genetic experiments, highly successful, are
greeted with criticism as well as approval. The criticism is not
ideological, but to do with what the narrator calls 'a feeling of
loss . . . when such deliberate, controlled experiments take place
. . . it is felt – most deeply and profoundly – . . . that some
other possibility may have been lost. As if randomness and
chance in themselves are a good and a blessing and even a
means of acquiring something not yet defined' (p. 59).
Throughout her narrative Ambien II shows her growing
awareness of the Canopean influence through statements of this
kind. Although Sirius regards Canopus as a colonial rival, and
has indeed fought and lost a war against her, Canopean
behaviour has always been magnanimous and honourable. After

the war they allow Sirius to stay on Rohanda, and do not justify the suspicions of the Sirians. Gradually, Ambien II realises that within the Canopean way of life lies something that will enable her to fulfil her own potential. Such wonderings are expressed tentatively at first: 'I felt about Canopus that inward, brooding, questioning, wondering, that one may sometimes feel about a person whose sources of action, of being, seem distant and other – as if understanding this being may open doors in oneself whose existence one does not do more than suspect' (pp. 85–6).

Ambien II welcomes the opportunity of working with a Canopean, Klorathy, and from him she absorbs more of the subtle, undidactic influence of Canopus. Haltingly, she formulates for herself the idea that she is being used for a purpose: the changing of Sirian ideas through her influence derived from Canopus. When Ambien II is able to say this to her co-rulers, she weeps, atavistic behaviour no longer practised by the Sirians. Then, having considered her role in effecting change on Sirius, she goes on to consider with her fellow rulers the mechanism of change as illustrated by examples from Rohanda/Shikasta/Earth. At this point Doris Lessing looks openly at the question that has been implicit from the beginning of the novel: what causes change in society? She uses as an example the report on the sinking of the *Titanic*, which was accepted as truthful at the time, and a few years later was condemned as mendacious whitewash. Why is this? What causes a change in viewpoint and values which then overturns previously held convictions? She gives a more dramatic example: 'millions will go to war for opinions that may very well be different or even opposite only a decade later – and die in their milions' (pp. 314–15). Through her narrator Mrs Lessing suggests that new ideas are brought into a group through a deviant individual who, if not thrown out of the group, will influence it. But the question remains, who or what influences the individual to deviate from the group's thinking? In this novel, it is Canopus who has influenced Ambien II, and predictably, she is sent on extended leave to another planet (a euphemism for house arrest). She writes an account of her experiences, giving it a punning title *The Sirian Experiments*, which is leaked to the Sirian people, ostensibly against the will of the co-rulers.

Nevertheless, the novel ends on a hopeful note. Ambien II, although officially unacceptable, is visited by each of her former co-rulers, separately. She realises that they are coming round to her way of thinking, and envisages meeting them together when they too are sent on extended leave to join her in exile. In other words, she is hopeful that her ideas will be disseminated through her colleagues to the populace of Sirius in general. The final message of *The Sirian Experiments* is that the influence of Canopus will prevail.

The novel is particularly interesting in relation to Mrs Lessing's own ability to absorb and transmit new ideas before they are generally received. From the accumulating evidence of her novels and other writings, it would seem that she believes that it is possible for individuals to 'tune in' to a higher consciousness, (possibly linked in her case with the practice of Sufi) which may alert an individual to what is about to happen. In *Canopus in Argos: Archives* this higher and altogether nobler level of thought emanates from the planet Canopus, and we are shown that those who come in touch with Canopus become aware of a need to change, although they often fight this. Of course, one can read *The Sirian Experiments* simply as a psychological metaphor about growth and openness to ideas. But Mrs Lessing means it to be taken more literally than this. She seems to be saying that perhaps we really are influenced for change by forces of which we are ignorant. And perhaps the peculiar truth of her fiction is a more subtle method than her clear statements in the preface, of conveying this belief to a materialist and sceptical population.

The Making of the Representative for Planet 8 is the fourth volume of *Canopus in Argos: Archives*. Planet 8 has been populated by a species bred by the Canopeans. During a visit from Johor, the emissary from Canopus, they are told to build a huge wall encircling their globe. They do this, without knowing what it is for. Eventually its purpose is made apparent. The climate of Planet 8 changes from temperate to freezing, and the wall is to withstand the force of ice which will otherwise cover the whole country. The Representatives, or leaders of the planet, understand that the population will be space-lifted off to Rohanda, to enjoy the benefits of easier climatic conditions. They see their task as enabling the people to withstand the ice and snow until they can be delivered from their slowly-dying planet. This is not easy, and the Representatives frequently ask themselves 'Where was Canopus?' When Johor returns, however, it is not with fleets of space craft to rescue them, but to tell them that Rohanda too is degenerating, and that they cannot be taken there after all. The narrator realises that when he relinquishes the old hope of being rescued, there is a strength inside him, unrelated to hopes and fears and promises. Finally, the Representatives lose their individual identities and 'the Representative' becomes a collective noun: 'this Being, we now were, – Johor with and of us, Johor mingled with us, the Representative of Canopus part of the Representative of Planet 8' (p. 159). The unmaking, the destruction of the planet, is in fact the making of the Representative. The narrator acknowledges that: 'We were learning, we old ones, that in times when a species, a race, is under threat, drives and necessities built into the very substance of our flesh speak out in ways that we need never have known about if extremities had not come to squeeze these truths out of us' (p. 38). The Representative finally transcends the limitations of the destroyed planet, mystically and without a space-craft to lift them off, just as the characters at the end of *The Memoirs of a Survivor* go through the wall into another world.

In this novel Mrs Lessing reiterates the necessity of the individual to realise that she or he is part of a collective spirit. Johor asks Doeg, the narrator: 'Do you believe that when you come to yourself from a world of dreams you think no one else shares, your consciousness of yourself, this feeling *I am here, Doeg is here* – belongs only to yourself, and no one else shares that feeling?' (p. 83). As Doeg comes to terms with the loss – or rather, the non-existence of the concept of the unique individual, he realises that it can be taken further. Looking at the delightful little snow creatures that are going to become extinct, he says 'you will say, Johor, that this charm, this delightfulness, will vanish here and reappear elsewhere. . . . It does not matter that they are going, the individual does not matter, the species does not matter' (p. 109). This relinquishing of the individual self is achieved by the characters, one by one. The girl, Alsi, says 'I am no longer Alsi' (p. 145), and this is echoed by the Representatives, who admit their redundancy on their own particular planet. The specific person, or genus, is irrelevant,

but something essential is retained, and has a role elsewhere:
'And then Klin, the Fruit Maker, the Guardian of the Orchards:
There is not one orchard or fruit tree or fruit anywhere in this
world of ours, nothing is left of all that beauty and richness –
and so Klin I am not, since Klin is what I did – Klin is at work
somewhere else' (p. 146). The hope of rescue (and with it the
retention of their own identities and roles to function elsewhere),
has to be abandoned, it would seem, for the spiritual growth of
the Representatives. It is only when they accept that they,
personally, may not fulfil their potential, that they are able to
transcend individual yearnings, individual aspirations, and
become part of a collective consciousness beyond the concept of
individuality.

The novel ends in a lyrical and mystical key. Mrs Lessing's
prose is unusually flowing, as if she were transcribing at great
speed some personal revelation about the true nature of spiritual
reality. (Indeed, this novel as a whole is exceptional in its stylistic
cohesion.) In a kind of dying vision, Doeg describes what he
and the other members of the Representative are finally able to
perceive. They see not only their planet as it has been, but also

> *possibilities*, what could have been, but had not been, in our
> space and time. But had been elsewhere? Yes, that was it, we
> were observing how, behind or beside or beyond – at any
> rate, some *where* or *when* – the various stages of development
> of our planet, had been so many others, the possibilities that
> had not been given actuality in the level of experience we had
> known, had experienced; but hovered just behind the veil,
> potentials, what might have been or could have been. . . .
> Myriads there were, the unachieved possibilities; but each
> real and functioning on its own level – *where* and *when* and
> *how?* – each world every bit as valid and valuable as what we
> had known as real. (p. 160)

This extract has been quoted at length as being central to an
understanding of Mrs Lessing's thinking at this point in her
canon. In this visionary passage she is giving validity to the
unrealised, to the richness of potentiality. Far from this being a
negative or quiescent version of actuality, she emphasises the
richness of the state of latency. Or rather, she suggests that what
might seem merely latent to us may have a 'functioning on its own

114 *Doris Lessing*

level' not comprehensible in our terms. This is one of Mrs Lessing's most interesting conclusions; it urges the mind to take in a scheme of being that does not consist merely of the tangible and hopes of being rescued from enmeshment in it. It is a schema which makes individual achievement a tiny part of a whole which encompasses all possibilities, physical as well as spiritual, even if they have not come to fruition as we understand it. This is a development from Mrs Lessing's increasingly urgent emphasis on the unimportance of the individual, a theme which has gathered momentum in her novels since *The Golden Notebook*. Up to now, she has insisted on the importance of the collective as opposed to the individual but here in *The Making of the Representative for Planet 8*, she goes further. If potential existence and achievement are given the same values as the actual states, then it scarcely matters whether they are actualised or not. The collective becomes not just a fusion of separate, actual egos but a state which includes innumerable potentialities, of which an individual ego is but a tiny manifestation.

It is a pity that Mrs Lessing did not end *Canopus in Argos: Archives* with *The Making of the Representative for Planet 8*, because both thematically and stylistically it has the sense of an ending and of a completion. We are left with Mrs Lessing's beautiful and visionary recognition of an evolutionary process in which ideas of mere individuality, of fulfilling one's personal destiny, of generic or global achievement are rejected. The process transcends these aims, which are seen as petty and limiting. At the end of this novel one is left with a curiosity similar to that felt at the end of *The Memoirs of a Survivor*: where can she go from here? *Memoirs* was followed, of course, by an imaginative leap unprecedented in Mrs Lessing's fiction; *The Making of the Representative for Planet 8* is followed by a repetitive reworking of material used in the preceding volumes of *Canopus in Argos: Archives*. Its tone is stale, and Mrs Lessing compounds its staleness with a kind of weary facetiousness, as if to try to enliven it. In *The Sentimental Agents in the Volyen Empire* – the last novel in the series – Mrs Lessing gives a close-up view of the degeneration of the Volyen Empire, and its invasion by Sirius. In some ways it is a recasting of issues explored in *Shikasta*, but whereas *Shikasta* was investigative in tone, *The Sentimental Agents* is wearily satirical.

Volyen is infiltrated by agents from Canopus, Sirius and Shammat, and the novel deals with their respective influences. Although the main action of the novel is the Sirian invasion of the Volyen Empire, Mrs Lessing's theme is the danger of oratory and rhetoric, and its power to stimulate false emotions causing impulsive and misguided action. A Canopean agent, Incent, succumbs to the influence of Shammat and is put into the Hospital for Rhetorical Diseases, where he is visited by his supervisor Klorathy. Examples of the danger of rhetoric are shown to him as part of his treatment, and Mrs Lessing uses the First World War as an illustration: 'Two vast armies . . . urged on by *words* used to inflame violent rival nationalism, each nation convinced, hypnotized by *words* to believe that it is in the right. Millions die, weakening both nations irreparably' (p. 19). Both Canopus and Shammat realise the power and the danger of rhetoric, but while Canopus tries to make its agents immune to it, Shammat exploits its lethal potential. Shammat has founded a School of Rhetoric on Volyen, in order to train propagandists to incite others to action: 'a school for the use of power over others, for the crude manipulation of the lowest instincts' (p. 87). Students are chosen from promising young orators, and are then taught to dissociate themselves from the emotions they inspire. To this end, examinations consist of emotive speeches, with the students wired up electronically to record their own emotional reaction to key words such as 'friends', 'work', 'comrades', 'sacrifice'. A buzzer sounds when the recorded reaction is over the prescribed limit, and then the student is failed.

As Judith Stitzel points out, Mrs Lessing has spoken elsewhere of the peculiarly disabling effect of certain words: 'This word "fascist" is one of the great words of the moment that stops everyone from thinking. You have only to say that so-and-so's a fascist and that's the end of any reason: you can't think after that'.[41] It is a theme to which she returns in *The Good Terrorist*, where her heroine Alice is shown to be totally mesmerised by the ritual use of political clichés. In *The Sentimental Agents in the Volyen Empire* she attacks some of the most sacred of contemporary rallying cries. In the Hospital for Rhetorical Diseases is a group of young people who are chanting:

> We shall overcome
> We shall overcome
> We shall overcome one day.

The narrator goes on to say 'The tune of this dirge originated V-millenniums ago on Volyen during its time as a Volyenadnan colony, to express the hopelessness of slaves' (p. 201). American critics, in particular, have been offended by this,[42] and it is indeed courageous of Doris Lessing to denigrate what was virtually the youth anthem of the 1960s. For her it is clearly a song of impotent, sentimental indulgence, and its emotive qualities are what she most dislikes. This links closely with her interest in Sufi, which encourages the practice of clear, objective perception. In a review of a book by Idries Shah, Mrs Lessing points out:

> We live in a society where emotionalism is prized; to say that something has moved us, is the equivalent of saying it is good, worthy, admirable. But the Sufis say that many of the 'higher' feelings we prize are merely crude emotionalism; and 'It is characteristic of the primitive to regard things which are felt strongly to be of importance.' And, again, 'the importance of something is in inverse proportion to its attractiveness'.[43]

By the end of this novel these points are hammered home through Mrs Lessing's repetition and heavy-handed jokes. (In *The Good Terrorist*, on the other hand, the dangers of emotionalism are treated with subtlety and wit.) Here there is a world-weariness in a literal sense which borders on cynicism, almost as if she is fatigued by offering yet another angle on human folly with the prior knowledge that it will not be acted upon. Her weariness makes this text more static and less dynamic than the earlier books of the Archive. My mind and emotions still resonate from the forays, the exploration, the risk-taking and the vision of the first four volumes; this one leaves me with a sense of staleness.

Nevertheless, viewed overall, *Canopus in Argos: Archives* is an extraordinary achievement. By taking the original and, for her, unusual step of moving into science fiction, Mrs Lessing moved into a genre which can encompass anything. All the prescriptions of realist fiction disappear. The sky is not the limit, and the divergence of points of view, time-scale, location and characterisation can have full play. This has great advantages both for writer and reader, since neither has to strain to accommodate such anomalies as the dog–cat creature, Hugo, in *The Memoirs of a Survivor*. In science fiction, anything can happen: and while Mrs Lessing's galaxies are carefully constructed systems, with detailed (and, in their own terms, logical) spatial and temporal descriptions, there is no reason why they should be. Mrs Lessing uses this freedom to deal with vital questions, and the novel series is in fact a detailed examination of the state of the planet Earth. In it she looks at our history, or rather, our cosmogony and the forces which have led to our present unhappy state. She examines the mechanisms of change, and its agents, and the possibility of transcendence. This last is important: if we understand this world according to Mrs Lessing, the logical desire, or even need, is to detach oneself from it, and to enter the realms inhabited by her enlightened characters. The adoption of space fiction exactly suits Mrs Lessing's beliefs, just as *The Golden Notebook* echoed her reservations about realism at that time. In *Canopus in Argos: Archives* she is dealing with unearthly, unworldly ideas, those more often expressed in philosophical or religious terms, and clearly she needs an extra-terrestial canvas on which to illustrate them in terms of fiction. She charts both inner and outer space, not simply as a record of her own explorations, but in the urgent hope that her maps will enable others to make their own journeys, their own discoveries. *Canopus in Argos: Archives* is, for all its calm tone, a didactic work, made powerful by the enormous moral confidence of its author. Although the cool vision of the archivist ostensibly disguises attitudes and bias, these novels, taken as a whole, blazon a warning. Mrs Lessing's recurrent theme is the disastrous course this planet seems set on, and the methods of coping with catastrophe. Seen in this light, *Canopus in Argos: Archives* becomes more than an esoteric work of fiction; read aright it may be, quite literally, a handbook for survival.

7

Return to Realism

The Diaries of Jane Somers – consisting of two novels by Doris Lessing called *The Diary of a Good Neighbour* and *If the Old Could* . . . – were published in 1984 and immediately caused a furore. This was because Mrs Lessing revealed that they had previously been published under a pseudonym, and almost totally ignored. The novels had been submitted to her publisher, Cape, and were turned down, and this elaborate joke at the expense of publishers' readers and literary critics was responsible for some ill-feeling against Mrs Lessing. She, however, is unrepentant. In the preface to *The Diaries of Jane Somers* she explains that she wanted to be reviewed on merit, 'without the benefit of a "name"' (p. 5). She also wanted to show that the process of rejection new, unknown authors go through is often mechanical, and not always related to the quality of the books they write. Finally, with what she admits was slight malice, she wanted to see if those reviewers who had hated the non-realism of *Canopus in Argos: Archives* would recognise her in her return to realistic fiction. No one did, and there is an undertone of glee in Mrs Lessing's account of her exploits as an unknown author.

She is very critical of the fact that the novels were not promoted because there was 'nothing to promote, no "personality", no photograph, no story' (Preface, p. 8). The publicity machine had nothing to feed it, and the merits of a first novel, she suggests, are seldom sufficient on their own to sell it. In the event, *The Diary of a Good Neighbour* sold 1600 copies in England and 2800 copies in America. Mrs Lessing then published a second novel under the pseudonym Jane Somers, entitled *If the Old Could* . . . which again was reviewed without the critics realising who the real author was. Not surprisingly, some critics have suggested that Mrs Lessing's motives are less straightforward than she makes out. Jonathan

Yardley accuses her of a publicity stunt,[44] and suggests that a real test of her experiment would have been to continue publishing under the pseudonym, rather than revealing herself after two novels. Ellen Goodman suggests that: 'Here is a woman who has spent her life wrestling with questions of who-am-I. It's unlikely that she would throw her name away for a cause. If she was toying with the book industry, I suspect that she was playing a more intriguing game with her own identity.'[45] She goes on to make the apt comparison with Kate Brown in *The Summer Before the Dark* where she walks past a building site without attracting any attention, and then accentuates her sexuality and walks back, causing wolf-whistles and comments. The pseudonymous author loses her public identity, and Ellen Goodman makes the point that Mrs Lessing was making an attempt to see if she 'existed' without her famous name: 'Life is too fragile if your identity is solely defined by others; it is hard, a life-long task to go on defining and redefining yourself.'[46] Whatever her motives, it was a courageous experiment, and one few authors are in a position to try. It confirms Mrs Lessing's great versatility, and her reluctance to be pinned down as one particular type of writer. Throughout her career she has explored a theme, incorporated it into her work, and moved on. Earlier themes may resonate through later novels, but Mrs Lessing changes her emphases and her opinions. This readiness to move on, to immerse herself in new fictive experiences, is one of her sources of creativity, and in *The Diaries of Jane Somers* she moves light years away from her galactic empires, back to twentieth-century London.

It comes as some relief to return to the solid realism of these novels after the ethereal quality of *Canopus in Argos: Archives*. Initially, the setting and the protagonist seem like those from a novel by Margaret Drabble or Angus Wilson: a clever, smart, middle-aged widow lives in a London flat furnished in expensive good taste. She works on an up-market woman's magazine and spends endless time and money on her clothes and her appearance. But although the theme is down to earth, so to speak, we may still find ourselves in new, unexplored areas: those of ageing, slow physical deterioration and death. Jane Somers becomes friendly with a very old woman called Maudie Fowler. Maudie lives in poverty and squalor, and finally dies of cancer in a geriatric hospital at the age of 92. The novel is a record of their friendship, and there is evidence that Mrs Lessing based it on someone she knew in real life. In a broadcast talk she mentions 'certain experiences I'd had with old people and with the social services in London'.[47] And in the Afterword to *The Making of the Representative for Planet 8* she writes that she finished it 'the day after the death of someone I had known a long time. . . . It took her a long cold time to die, and she was hungry too, for she was refusing to eat and drink, so as to hurry things along. She was ninety-two, and it seemed to her sensible' (p. 189). It is an extraordinarily convincing portrait of a proud, touchy old person, who has flashes of sweetness and charm, but who is totally unsentimentalised by Mrs Lessing.

The emphasis in *The Diaries of Jane Somers* is on ageing and its consequent drawbacks. Mrs Lessing details with horrible clarity the sordid physical difficulties involved in being old and ill, and in an interesting review Carey Kaplan notes how these novels interlock with the *Canopus* quintet. In the space fiction series the emphasis is on immortality: 'Time's power is denied. Part of Canopus's superiority is that used parts can be replaced with new perfect ones. Canopean agents live forever, remote from such vulgarities as coitus, defecation, indigestion, or death.'[48] Whereas *The Diaries* are full of these things; the shadow side, if you like, of the disembodied Canopeans. Indeed, *The Diary of a Good Neighbour* reinforces the Swiftian note of physical disgust which runs through Mrs Lessing's novels from *The Four-Gated City* onwards. As she increasingly appreciates mankind's spiritual dimension, she separates it from our animality, almost as if she cannot accommodate the two in one human being. There is a great deal about defecation in this novel, since Maudie Fowler is often doubly incontinent. Janna bravely washes her, and the stench makes her feel sick. In her diary she cannot pretend to be neutral about it, and through Maudie she faces the horrors of old age. She tries to take her imagination one step further, and to look at her own death.

I imagine, deliberately, all kinds of panic, of dread: I make myself visualize me, Janna, sitting up on high pillows, very old, being destroyed from within. I reduce my outer boundaries back, back, first from my carapace of clothes, how I present myself; and then to my healthy body, which does not – yet – suddenly let loose dirt and urine against my will, but is still comely and fresh; and back inside, to me, the knowledge of I, and imagine how it is a carcass I am sitting in, that's all, a slovenly mess of meat and bones. But it is no good. I do not fear death. I do not. (p. 242)

Later in the novel Janna herself has a bad attack of lumbago, and is unable to move. She is immobilised in bed, and has to be nursed: 'a routine was established – around the animal's needs. The animal has to get rid of x pints of liquid and half a pound of shit; the animal has to ingest so much liquid and so much cellulose and calories' (p. 139). This helplessness enables her to share Maudie's experience, and one of the strengths of this novel is the emphasis on imaginative identification. Mrs Lessing makes Janna work to increase her empathy with Maudie. At one point Janna writes in her diary an account of a day from Maudie's point of view, in order to try to understand her better. She stresses the sheer physical difficulties and slowness of body maintenance, of eating and drinking, sleeping and excreting, which expand to fill the whole day. In contrast, Janna's account of the same day from her own point of view omits these references, simply because they take up so little time and seem relatively unimportant compared with her busy working life. The novel also includes an account of a day in the life of a Home Help, which seems extraordinarily accurate both in mood and in factual detail.

In her earlier novels, the narrator's viewpoint has almost always been close to that of Mrs Lessing; her protagonists resemble her. Here, through the persona of Janna, who does not resemble her, she explores totally different life-styles and types. Mrs Lessing has said of this novel 'I wanted to write it in the first person. I found something rather interesting: Jane Somers is very English. I mean, she is *very*, *very* English. . . . when I was inside the skin of Jane Somers, I found my whole world getting very narrow.'[49] She makes Jane, or Janna, obsessive about her immaculate appearance and her beautiful flat, and admits that Janna would have found Doris a threat: 'People like me – who have very little structure to their lives, who are untidy, apparently disorderly, and who are unable to decide what is wrong and what is right – make these people feel very upset, and they tend to avoid us.'[50] Janna's carefully maintained life-style serves to accentuate the great contrast between herself and Maudie Fowler. But from her exploration into Maudie's past, Jane manages to close the gap by evoking her as a young girl: wearing a new dress, being courted, working as a milliner. From her initial perception of her as a lonely, stubborn, dirty old woman, Janna comes to appreciate the richness of Maudie's past life. And in coping with Maudie's final illness and death, Janna realises that she had previously made herself immune to the death of her mother and her husband, and especially, to the prospect of her own. In the geriatric hospital where she dies, Maudie and her fellow patients become a *memento mori* for Janna: 'Once I was so afraid of old age, of death, that I refused to let myself see old people in the streets – they did not exist for me. Now, I sit for hours in that ward and watch and marvel and wonder and admire' (p. 245). The fear of becoming old is expressed in 1956, in *Retreat to Innocence*: 'An old woman came towards her. Julia watched her, appalled. "Imagine being old. Imagine when no one will turn to look at me . . . It must be like being a ghost, moving among other people, and no one noticing you at all"' (Ch. 2). In *The Diary of a Good Neighbour* her experience with Maudie breaks down Janna's self-sufficiency and self-absorption. She no longer has time for her long, scented baths or maintaining her expensive wardrobe. As she allows her smooth façade to show cracks, Janna is able to examine her troubled relationship with her sister's family, and how her sister bore the brunt of nursing their mother before her death. Jane is then able to invite one of her nieces to live with her, to their mutual benefit and pleasure.

The Diary of a Good Neighbour is about shedding protective layers and changing direction. Maudie, for all her pride, gradually allows Janna to get closer to her, and admits – haltingly, grudgingly – that she likes her company. Janna's relationship with Maudie brings her in touch with all the methods she has used in the past to insulate herself from feeling, and its attendant risk of feeling pain. With the exception of Muriel Spark, there are few contemporary writers who have dealt so powerfully with the taboo topic of growing old. We are not spared the sordid and sometimes grotesque details, and it is typical of Mrs Lessing (albeit that this is a reversion to realism) that she is still charting territory beyond the confines of the commonplace imagination.

The sequel to *The Diary of a Good Neighbour* was also published under the pseudonym of Jane Somers, and called *If the Old Could* . . . The title is taken from a French proverb: 'If the young knew . . . If the old could . . .' It is the story of a love affair between Janna Somers and a man called Richard Curtis, whom she meets by accident in London. He is married, with strong family commitments, and he and Janna have an unconsummated love affair, during the course of a summer. The couple are dogged by two neurotic teenagers, Richard's daughter Kathleen, and Jane's niece Kate, both of whom follow them jealously. To add to their difficulties, Janna perversely falls in love with Matthew, Richard's son. He has stolen from his father a photograph of her as a girl, and when they meet he says 'I love you, Janna', words she has longed to hear from Richard. She is horrified at her reaction: 'That rather unpleasant young man put his finger on some unknown part of me that had been programmed to hear just those words and no other: Wow! Blam! I fell in love. I am poisoned. I am possessed by a sickly sweet fever. I am obsessed' (p. 469). This makes her unable to see Richard for three weeks, but they resume their relationship before he returns to America, where he lives. There is very little action in this novel, but the painful hopelessness and the joy of their love affair is evoked strongly, and is all the more poignant because the lovers are both in their fifties and conscious of their lost youth and lost opportunities.

Janna's feeling for Richard makes her realise that she never loved her husband Freddie, who died of cancer. Paradoxically, this realisation makes her miss him badly, and she dreams of him and of being in love with him as she was not in real life. With Freddie she had a good relationship, but her friendship with Richard is platonic. When they plan to spend a night together, the atmosphere is disastrous, and they realise that sex will somehow be detrimental to their association. This does not diminish their love, however, and in this novel Mrs Lessing endows the affair with some of her most lyrical writing. She is not usually given to flights of beautiful, fluid prose. Her style is functional, and her imagination is used, as it were, for practical purposes, such as the description of events from two or three different viewpoints. In *If the Old Could* . . . there is a passage totally unlike her normal style. Describing her love affair, Janna says:

I feel in a sudden and amazing surge of love and happiness
the truth of being with Richard. Which can best be expressed,
quite simply, thus: There is nothing we could not say to each
other, as if our two lives, running for so long invisibly to the
other and coming together so improbably in that comic little
accident on Tottenham Court Road underground, carried
along with them a rich cargo that had been invisible, too, to
ourselves, like rivers whose depths know nothing about the
baulks of good timber, green boughs from some far-off flood
in the mountains, packing cases that have who knows what
things in them – silks? books? special scented teas from North
India? a consignment of rare plants from some jungle destined
for a garden in Northern Europe? seventeen disconsolate
chickens sitting on a bucking and rearing log, a drowned
horse, and the light worn bones of an ancient dinosaur that
has been washed off some eroding hillside. All these things,
carried along so far by the flood, swirl into a side-reach of the
river, toss a little, and subside in brown froth on a beach of
white sand whose river waves run past in a normal season
smooth and orderly, each modestly crested with white.
(p. 370)

This flight of fancy juxtaposes both the romantic and the
prosaic elements of their two separate lives, and the mention of
dinosaur bones evokes a sense of past time, as if the meeting
had been destined for millions of years. Words such as 'rich',
'good', 'scented', 'rare' suggest the quality of their present
relationship, which is not diminished by the admission of the
humorous and the grotesque: 'seventeen disconsolate chickens'
and 'a drowned horse'. The phrase 'carried along by the flood'
reflects Janna's feelings for Richard, and even the structure of
this passage – two long, flowing sentences – echoes the metaphor
of the two rivers. In this kind of writing it is as if Mrs Lessing
has stopped striving for the appropriate words, has relaxed and
allowed the images to float into her conscious mind, like a poet
at moments of inspiration. The result is just as authentic as a
careful delineation of the love affair, and indeed, essentially
more truthful.

Throughout both volumes of *The Diaries of Jane Somers* there is
emphasis on Janna's work as a powerful assistant editor on a
women's magazine. This involves trips abroad for fashion shows

and conferences, and she makes sure that she maintains an immaculate appearance. In addition she has a niece living with her, and regularly visits two or three old ladies, cleaning and shopping for them, making them clothes and washing them. She also writes a novel in her spare time. Janna is very proud of her ability to get things done, and there is an almost puritanical emphasis on work in these novels, as if it were a cohesive agent in a life which might otherwise fall apart. In *The Diary of a Good Neighbour* Janna's niece Jill comes to live with her, and works, very successfully, on the magazine. The two live together, contentedly, both hard-working, neat, practical and elegant. In *If the Old Could* . . . Jill's sister Kate replaces her, and is in absolute contrast to Jill's efficiency and vitality. Kate is lazy and dirty. She is plugged into pop music all day, and although she is 19, she has no plans to study or get a job. She makes the acquaintance of some young people living in a squat, who deliberately mess up Janna's flat while she is away. The relationship between aunt and niece is analogous to that between Janna and the old people she visits; they are demanding, difficult and ungrateful, and yet she recognises some desperate need in them, and perhaps in herself, for affection and companionship. Kate and the old people act as a balance and a corrective to the heady, glamorous magazine world Janna works in, almost as if their squalor counteracts any tendency Janna might have to lose touch with the everyday world.

The unredeemed awfulness of Kate is unconvincing, especially when teamed with Richard's similarity difficult daughter Kathleen. The clash between the censorious younger generation and their elders reminds me of Mrs Lessing's play *Each His Own Wilderness* (1959). In this play a middle-aged woman is criticised by her son for her involvement in politics, for her love affairs, and in general for her way of life which he feels is inappropriate to her age. I am moved that Mrs Lessing's middle-aged characters do not grow old gracefully, but are still falling in love, still experimenting, still making mistakes. In this novel Janna is amazed at the strength and newness of her feelings for Richard, but is still accepting and learning from this unprecedented experience. In her review of *The Diaries of Jane Somers* Carey Kaplan says 'Doris Lessing may yet give us a fully integrated glimpse of the world of old age in which one's own body − insistent and failing − becomes repulsive; in which

youthful struggle seems ludicrous; in which helplessness must
be accepted; in which a lifetime seems a minute; in which the
necessity for resignation becomes inevitable.'[51] Perhaps she will,
but she has not done so yet. The Canopean world transcends
old age and helplessness; Jane Somer's world incorporates them
with such vitality that resignation, however appropriate, would
seem to be an admission of failure.

In 1985 Mrs Lessing published another realistic novel, again
set in London. It is about a group of terrorists, living in a
squat. This is a house purchased by the council for
redevelopment, and deliberately made uninhabitable to prevent
squatters moving in. After due negotiation with the authorities,
services are restored, and the group are allowed to live there,
rent-free, providing they pay gas and electricity charges and
water rates. The complex arrangements for all this are made by
Alice Mellings. She is a woman in her mid-thirties who has had
no job since she graduated, but for fifteen years has shared her
life with a man called Jasper, moving from place to place. They
are not lovers, because Jasper is homosexual, but they have a
symbiotic relationship based on a reluctant mutual need. The
novel charts Alice's role as 'mother' of the household, and
examines the political motivations and rhetoric of the group.
Alice makes soup downstairs, while another girl makes bombs
upstairs. The group calls itself the Communist Centre Union,
and has grandiose plans for violent revolution, seeking to assist
the IRA. After a successful trial run in blowing up a bollard,
they bomb a luxury hotel in London, killing five people and
injuring twenty-three others.
    As in *The Diaries of Jane Somers* Mrs Lessing covers new
ground in her subject matter, this time exploring the urban
terrorism which is an intrinsic aspect of the 1980s. She does so
with a similar emphasis on the sheer mechanics of everyday
living, but unlike that of the *Diaries* the tone of this novel is
powerfully ironic. The grotesque paradox throughout is Alice's
efforts to make habitable a house and to care for the well-being
of her fellow terrorists, in order that they may blast other
buildings and other human beings to pieces. The juxtaposition
of Alice's yen and capacity for creating cosy domesticity, and
her commitment to terrorism, is ludicrous and frequently very

funny. This is Mrs Lessing's most savage novel, as though she has suddenly and finally lost patience with the effort of hoping that the younger generation might build on the painfully learnt political lessons of their elders.

The characterisation of Alice, the protagonist of this novel, is marvellously well done. She is a successor to Kate in *If the Old Could* . . ., although without Kate's miserable lethargy. Neither has the ability to think for herself, and both long for acceptance and gratitude from a group in order to achieve an identity, if only vicariously. And, like Kate, Alice cannot acknowledge her sexuality, which she has long suppressed. Mrs Lessing indicates this in a moving passage which contrasts strongly with the frequent descriptions of Alice's practical activities:

> her fingers were sliding over the satiny warmth of her skin, and in a sweet intimate flash of reminder, or of warning, her body (her secret breathing body which she ignored for nearly all of her time, trying to forget it) came to life and spoke to her. Her fingers were tingling with the warm smoothness, and she stood there looking puzzled . . . over that message from her buried self. (p. 198)

And when she finds some antique evening dresses in the attic, she begins to try one on, but tears it off quickly, 'as if she had been tempted briefly by the forbidden' (p. 154). Alice's creativity is expressed through her ability to turn a stinking neglected house into a comfortable home smelling of newly baked bread and fresh flowers. Mrs Lessing's technical knowledge of how to organise a squat is very impressive, and much of the novel is taken up with descriptions of Alice's expertise: methods of dealing with council departments; organising guarantors in order to have electricity and gas and water reconnected; burying buckets of excrement in the garden; finding cheap labour to make the wiring safe and the lavatories usable; obtaining discarded but adequate furniture from skips; buying a second-hand gas boiler and water tank; stealing money from her family in order to pay for it all. Alice's work on the house is genuinely creative, as is her pleasure in caring for others, and making things run smoothly. But these skills are perverted, since she exercises them in a kind of mad isolation: they are reserved only for the service of people who exploit her, and treat her badly. Her parents, and 'society' are seen as the enemy, and as such, are subject to the bitterest contempt.

What is so extraordinary about Alice (and indeed, all the terrorists) is their inability to make any connection between cause and effect, action and consequences. Thus Alice is totally unable to understand that her mother has had to move into a tiny, ugly flat because Jasper and Alice have sponged off her for four years. And, having bankrupted her mother, had a blazing row with her and walked out of the house, Alice is able, three hours later, to ask her to guarantee the electricity and gas payments for the squat. Alice steals a thousand pounds from her father's firm, and is amazed and furious when suspicion naturally falls on the newest employee, a young black man who was given the job by Alice's father at her request. The essential quality for any terrorist is lack of imagination, since this would relate violent action to its appalling consequences, and become a deterrent. And even at the final recce before planting the bomb, Alice cannot make the final connection between the action and its consequences: 'Alice was thinking: but people might be *killed* . . . oh no, that couldn't happen! But inside her chest a pressure was building up, painful, like a cry – but she could not let it be heard' (p. 351). In this novel Mrs Lessing shows how the terrorists keep themselves encapsulated in solipsism, as if aware that knowledge of other people would be a contamination that might infect or dilute their political views.

Apart from the vague term 'revolution', it is difficult to see what the squatters are in favour of. Mrs Lessing wryly illustrates how a generalised concern for the masses frequently excludes help or kindness for specific individuals. A lesbian feminist called Faye attacks a desperate, homeless mother and baby who want to join the squat. A frail young man called Philip does most of the essential labour on the house, while the others (apart from Alice) are out enjoying themselves on picket lines or demonstrations. He is taken for granted by the commune and dies in an accident because he has lost the will to live. Alice is used by everyone, but takes this as a matter of course. With one or two exceptions, the squatters are selfish and rapacious, and their rhetoric on behalf of the oppressed proletariat is made ludicrous by their own actions.

Rhetoric is one of Mrs Lessing's principal satiric targets in this novel. In *Children of Violence* she makes clear her awareness that jargon is frequently used in place of thought, and in *The Good Terrorist* she reiterates this theme. The squatters' allegiance to the Communist Centre Union dictates their modes of speech. When they remember they call each other 'Comrade', and 'Fascist' is used indiscriminately as a word of abuse. Mrs Lessing's mockery is given great scope in her description of a meeting of the CCU. Jasper makes a speech consisting of catch-phrases strung together:

We all know the criminal, the terrible condition of Britain. We all know the fascist imperialist government must be forcibly overthrown! There is no other way forward! The forces that will liberate us are already being forged. We are in the vanguard of these forces, and the responsibility for a glorious future is with us, in our hands. (p. 220)

When one of the squatters is accused of stealing a car, he is upset: ' "We are revolutionaries," said Bert, furious. "Not crooks" ' (p. 278). The strong ironic tone within the novel is not the only corrective to the absurdities described. Alice's mother, Dorothy, spells out the sheer stupidity of the squatters. Her words carry some weight, because she too has been a communist, and her ire is not directed only at Alice, but at a friend and contemporary, Zoë. When Zoë comments that Dorothy no longer goes on demonstrations, she replies: ' "I'll tell you something, Zoë. All you people, marching up and down and waving banners and singing pathetic little songs – all you need is love; you are just a joke. They watch you at it and think: Good, that's keeping them busy" ' (p. 335). This is strong stuff, but it is a viewpoint that Mrs Lessing has already expressed in *Canopus in Argos: Archives*. *The Good Terrorist* seems to indicate the end of her fictive concern with political commitment as begun in *Martha Quest*. It is not, as some critics have indicated, that Mrs Lessing has become right-wing, but that she seems to have abandoned hope in politics as an effective means of change. In *The Good Terrorist* Dorothy knows that for the members of the CCU change simply means 'how to get power for yourselves' (p. 330). *Canopus in Argos: Archives* made clear that genuine change has first to be effected in oneself before it can be effected in society. In this novel, Dorothy Melling is freed from her marriage, her large house, her famous parties, her middle-aged daughter. Despite her poverty, she enjoys her new simplicity. She sits in her small flat and says '"It's fine. The simpler the better. When I think, the years of my life I've spent *fussing*"' (p. 328). Dorothy makes friends with an elderly working-class neighbour, and at last finds the courage to refuse to accept the responsibility of her daughter's prolonged immaturity.

The Good Terrorist does not deny the aspects of the twentieth century that so incense the squatters; modern urban architecture, lunatic bureaucracy, an increasingly embittered and violent police force: all these are described with accuracy and without surprise. But what the novel then goes on to do is to show the criminal naïvety of the extremists who believe that they are going to change the system they so deplore. In Mrs Lessing's view, the terrorists are part of contemporary dis-ease, and not a means of curing it. Somehow *The Good Terrorist* ought to be more depressing than it is, but Mrs Lessing's humour gives it a compulsive vitality. She sees through the cant, the slogans, the games-playing, and she has the integrity not to blur the clarity of her vision in her fiction for the sake of appeasement. She has been saying unpopular things for a long time now, and because she is both an artist and a visionary no doubt she will go on doing so.

Conclusion

Doris Lessing's contribution to the development of the novel is twofold: both her techniques and her subject-matter have broken boundaries and, as has been suggested, these are closely inter-related. The novel form has never been monolithic: in *Tristram Shandy*, for example, Laurence Sterne set up an alternative to realism before the realistic mode became established. Nevertheless, we tend in thinking of 'the novel' to take the nineteenth-century classic realist text as our model. And, in each generation, there are those writers who set out to subvert the realist tradition, to show how it is inadequate for their own particular time, to find out other ways of conveying their perceptions of what constitutes reality. Doris Lessing is such a writer for our times. She has taken risks, changed and moved on in her life, and this change and growth is reflected in her novels. Sometimes they follow a trend which she herself has signposted to the reader, and at other times they are utterly surprising, taking us into regions that are unexplored and uncharted. At the beginning of her canon she writes about the external world, but her protagonists are endowed with a sense of quest rather than acceptance or stasis. Gradually the search moves inwards, and she turns her attention to a study of the Sufi religion for confirmation of her belief that we are all part of a consciousness which both transcends and unifies the separateness of individuality. Most of her later novels are to do with her psychical development, and there is a sense that the writing is part of this experience. Her struggle (and sometimes her acknowledged failure) to find the right words to delineate a process or feeling or intuition is often a way of discovering more deeply the perceptions being described. For example, at the stage in her work when she becomes dissatisfied with realism she was becoming aware of the so-called 'real' world as superficial, aware also that her new insights could not be accommodated within the conventions of mimetic writings. So she moved towards reflexive fiction, examining the possibilities of truth-telling within the novel.

The Golden Notebook epitomised a phase of the post-modernist concern about the novel form, and it did so in a peculiarly 'English' way. That is to say that Mrs Lessing did not start from theoretical assumptions but from experience. She needed a new form because she found, through trial and error, that the old one could not accommodate her multi-layered version of reality. Lorna Sage puts it better:

> Because Lessing had found a form that so exactly focused her struggles with/against realism, it was a novel that persuaded its readers of the limitations of that shared language more painfully, and even perhaps more intimately, than French new novels, or than anti-realist writing from America. Sarraute and Robbe-Grillet began from the culture of the unreal, the sub-real; Barth and Pynchon were reflexive jokers from the start. But Lessing worked her passage, as it were, and documented the voyage. And the result was that she did what many of her 'experimental' contemporaries claimed, but failed to do – produced a novel that unravelled itself in its readers' responses in altogether unexpected ways. She had 'represented' them better than she knew.[52]

In its subject-matter *The Golden Notebook* dealt in detail with subjects that were previously taboo in English literature: women talking with unprecedented freedom about their attitudes to men; menstruation; vaginal versus clitoral orgasm. Above all, it initiated aspects of the feminist debate that were to become central issues in the years to come. This accurate anticipation of cultural trends, of the movement of the collective unconscious, makes Mrs Lessing extraordinarily powerful as a novelist. It is one of the reasons why, although she causes irritation and impatience by her detached and rather elevated world view, she cannot be dismissed simply as crazy. The accuracy of *The Golden Notebook* in representing its time, both technically and thematically, stands as a warning against ignoring Doris Lessing when she writes about the acute danger this planet is in, and possible methods of survival.

After *The Golden Notebook*, which is a watershed, Mrs Lessing felt free to abandon realism as and when she needed to. Subsequent novels encompass both the world that can be described realistically, and the other world that defies realistic description, that is, those areas of experience which are spiritual or transcendental. *Landlocked* and *The Four-Gated City* are basically realistic, but the subject-matter includes the non-rational, and in writing about it, Mrs Lessing feels free to abandon conventional sentence structure and a logical, progressive sequence of events. The novels are fluid, moving between physical and spiritual worlds, and their language reflects this fluidity. *Briefing for a Descent into Hell* can be accounted for in realistic terms, but by this time it is clear that Mrs Lessing's emphasis is on the psychical aspects of reality. In *The Memoirs of a Survivor* she drops all pretence of a realistic framework. The wall of the narrator's flat is both solid and permeable, literal and metaphorical, being also the wall between her awareness of a higher level of consciousness and her everyday life. At the end of this novel the wall dissolves completely, and it is not surprising that Doris Lessing moves out of this world for her next five novels. To accommodate the strangeness of her ideas without making excessive demands on realism, she set *Canopus in Argos: Archives* in the realms of science fiction, where the non-rational is the norm, and where she could safely write extraordinary truths without being criticised for straining realism beyond its limits. Anything is allowed in science fiction; like the court jester, a writer in this genre may tell (often unpalatable) truths under the protective guise of wild imaginings.

It is important, however, that the reader understands that Mrs Lessing's non-realist fiction is not regarded by her as pure fantasy. (Included in this category are *Briefing for a Descent into Hell* and *The Memoirs of a Survivor* as well as *Canopus in Argos: Archives*.) She is not an imaginative or inventive writer in the sense that she can conjure up worlds she has not experienced. That is to say that all her novels, without exception, are closely related to her own life, and that even the space fiction is a version of her spiritual growth and the perceptions which accompany it. She is not so much a creative writer as a chronicler of events: it is just that she has travelled further in psychical terms than most of us, and what she describes as the view in sight may seem like sheer invention to the traveller who has not reached that point, or, indeed, who has not even begun the journey. It is only when we ourselves reach the same viewpoint that we realise that she is not writing fiction, but an allegorical version of the facts.

After *Canopus in Argos: Archives* Mrs Lessing moves back to realism for *The Diaries of Jane Somers*, and this freedom of movement between genres is unparalleled by any of her contemporaries. She has made of the novel form what she wants it to be at any particular time, and this way of using the novel instead of being used by it, so to speak, puts a new perspective on the role of the novelist in relation to the form. Indeed, this view of the novel form being at her disposal links with her views on novels as disposable. At the end of the 1971 preface to *The Golden Notebook* she says:

> it is not only childish of a writer to want readers to see what he sees, to understand the shape and aim of a novel as he sees it – his wanting this means that he has not understood a most fundamental point. Which is that the book is alive and potent and fructifying and able to promote thought and discussion *only* when its plan and shape and intention are not understood, because that moment of seeing the plan and intention is also the moment when there isn't anything more to be got out of it. And when a book's pattern and the shape of its inner life is as plain to the reader as it is to the author – then perhaps it is time to throw the book aside, as having had its day, and start again on something new. (p. 22)

Novels, therefore, are not icons to be revered. Novels are disposable, she suggests, and their purpose is to make their authors redundant, and their readers move on.

Doris Lessing's critical reputation is very high. *The Grass is Singing* was immediately recognised as an exceptional novel on its publication in 1950, and her fame has gained steadily ever since. She is particularly respected in the United States of America, where the feminist and visionary aspects of her work were appreciated earlier than they were in Britain. Her books are widely translated, and she is recognised internationally as a committed novelist dealing with serious issues. She is famous, and it could well be that it was an attempt to find out how far her name enhances her reputation that led her to publish two novels under a pseudonym. She was scathing about the failure of critics to notice the novels, and her opinion of literary critics has never been very favourable. In *The Golden Notebook* preface she asks 'Why are they so parochial, so personal, so small-minded? Why do they always atomise, and belittle, why are they so fascinated by detail, and uninterested in the whole?' (p. 18). This study has tried to concentrate on the whole, and to show how Doris Lessing's own search for coherence is a theme which unites her novels. But I have become increasingly aware of a contradiction, a tension running through her work between the assured, confident voice of the author as shown through her narrators, and a subtext of what can only be called the voice of an unloved child crying for affection. It seems that there are two personae beneath the surface of these novels: the lofty, distant and serene adult who has asked the real questions and found many of the answers, and who lives in the cool Canopus air; and the insecure child-like figure, evidently mortal, anxious still about its identity, deeply disappointed that its own pain has had so little effect: 'That humanity was unable to learn from experience was written there for everyone to see, since the new generation of the intelligent and consciously active youth behaved identically with every generation before them.'[53] The bitterness of this realisation comes through in some of the later novels, undermining their surface serenity. And the unloved child comes through too, but is unacknowledged except in *The Memoirs of a Survivor*. This is Doris Lessing's best novel, precisely because of its admission of that child, who is given space along with the mature and wise adult.

The message of Doris Lessing's fiction is apocalyptic. She sees this planet as being in great danger of destruction, and in her novels she suggests two ways in which to deflect this danger. The first is to try to discover why ideas change – the mechanism of the *Zeitgeist* – so that we may utilise them rather than be swept along by them. The second is to be aware that we all have potentialities which in most of us are only partially evolved – such as telepathy and extra-sensory perception – which if developed may enable us to avert or survive a nuclear holocaust. For Mrs Lessing these are not simply *literary* concerns, not just exciting and interesting themes for a novelist to play

with, but some of her most deeply held beliefs. They are
expressed in a literary form, and they do entertain us, but they
should not be dismissed as pure fiction for all that. Long ago
Doris Lessing decided that fiction could be a medium for
expressing profound truths. Perhaps we should listen to what
she is saying before it is too late.

Notes

1. Interview with Roy Newquist, *Counterpoint* (Chicago, Ill.; Rand McNally, 1964), reprinted in *A Small Personal Voice*, ed. Paul Schlueter (New York: Vintage Books, 1975), pp. 45–60.

2. Doris Lessing, 'My Father', *Sunday Telegraph*, 1 September 1963, reprinted in *A Small Personal Voice*, pp. 83–93.

3. Ibid., p. 91. Doris Lessing writes in more detail about her mother in 'Impertinent Daughters', *Granta*, 14 (Winter 1984), 51–68, and 'Autobiography (Part Two): My Mother's Life', *Granta*, 17 (Autumn 1985), 227–38.

4. Lorna Sage, *Doris Lessing* (London: Methuen, 1983), p. 22.

5. Doris Lessing, Afterword to *The Story of an African Farm* by Olive Schreiner (New York: Fawcett World Library, 1968), reprinted in *A Small Personal Voice*, pp. 97–120.

6. 'A Conversation with Doris Lessing (1966)' (interview with Florence Howe), *Contemporary Literature*, 14, no. 4 (Autumn 1973), reprinted in *Doris Lessing: Critical Studies*, ed. Annis Pratt and L. S. Dembo (Madison: Univ. of Wisconsin Press, 1974), pp. 1–19.

7. 'Doris Lessing at Stony Brook: An interview by Jonah Raskin', first published in *New American Review*, 8 (New York: New American Library, 1970). Reprinted in *A Small Personal Voice*, pp. 61–76.

8. Elizabeth Wilson, 'Yesterday's Heroines: On Rereading Lessing and de Beauvoir', from *Notebooks/memoirs/archives: Reading and Rereading Doris Lessing*, ed. Jenny Taylor (London: Routledge and Kegan Paul, 1982), pp. 57–73.

9. 'An Evening at 92nd Street Y', Roberta Rubenstein, 'Reports: Lessing in North America, March–April, 1984; *Doris Lessing Newsletter*, 8, no. 2 (Fall 1984) 6.

10. Doris Lessing talking at the University of East Anglia, UK, 1980. (Unpublished transcript.)

11. Doris Lessing in a letter to Roberta Rubenstein, quoted in her book *The Novelistic Vision of Doris Lessing: Breaking the Forms of Consciousness* (Urbana: Univ. of Illinois Press, 1979), p. 231.

12. Ibid., p. 197.

13. Ibid., p. 198.

14. Idries Shah, *The Sufis* (New York: Doubleday, 1964), p. 61.

15. Doris Lessing, quoted by Nancy Shields Hardin in 'Doris Lessing and the Sufi Way', from *Doris Lessing: Critical Studies*, p. 153.

16. Especially the writers who gave the following papers at the Short Story Symposium at the College of St Paul and St Mary, Cheltenham, UK, in

137

138 *Notes*

September 1986: Ellen Cronan Rose, 'Crystals, Fragments and Golden Wholes: Short Stories in *The Golden Notebook*'; Claire Sprague, '"A Man and Two Women" and *The Golden Notebook*'; Virginia Tiger, 'Taking Hands and Dancing in (Dis)Unity'.

17. Anthony Chennells, 'Doris Lessing: Rhodesian Novelist', *Doris Lessing Newsletter*, 9, no. 2 (Fall 1985), 3–7.

18. Doris Lessing, 'A Deep Darkness: A Review of *Out of Africa* by Karen Blixen, *New Statesman*, 15 January 1971, pp. 87–8. Reprinted in *A Small Personal Voice*, pp. 147–52.

19. 'The Persistent Personal Voice: Lessing on Rhodesia and Marxism', interview with Eve Bertelsen, *Doris Lessing Newsletter*, 9, no. 2 (Fall 1985), 8, 9, 10, 18.

20. C. J. Driver, 'Doris Lessing', an interview in *The New Review*, 1, no. 8 (November 1974), 17–23.

21. Doris Lessing, 'The Small Personal Voice' in *Declarations*, ed. T. Maschler (London: MacGibbon and Kee, 1957), reprinted in *A Small Personal Voice*, pp. 3–21.

22. Nicole Ward Jouve, 'Of Mud and Other Matter – The Children of Violence' in *Notebooks/Memoirs/Archives*, pp. 75–134.

23. 'A Conversation with Doris Lessing' (interview with Florence Howe), *Doris Lessing: Critical Studies*, p. 8.

24. Quoted by Idries Shah in *The Way of the Sufi* (London: Cape, 1968; Harmondsworth: Penguin, 1974), p. 106.

25. Ibid., p. 20.

26. Barbara Hill Rigney, *Madness and Sexual Politics in the Feminist Novel: Studies in Brontë, Woolf, Lessing and Atwood* (Madison, Wisc.: Univ. of Wisconsin Press, 1978), p. 77.

27. Lorna Sage, *Doris Lessing*, pp. 67–8.

28. 'A Conversation with Doris Lessing' (interview with Florence Howe), *Doris Lessing: Critical Studies*, p. 11.

29. C. J. Driver, 'Doris Lessing', interview in *The New Review*, 1, no. 8 (November 1974), 22.

30. Marion Vlastos, 'Doris Lessing and R. D. Laing: Psychopolitics and Prophecy', *PMLA*, 91, no. 2 (March 1976), 245–58, and Roberta Rubenstein in *The Novelistic Vision of Doris Lessing*, p. 179.

31. Doris Lessing, interview with Roy Newquist, in *A Small Personal Voice*, p. 59.

32. Marilyn Ferguson, *The Aquarian Conspiracy: Personal and Social Transformation in the 1980s* (London: Routledge and Kegan Paul, 1981). This is a very useful book to read alongside Doris Lessing's later novels since it describes similar developments in human transformation.

33. Doris Lessing, interview with Susan Stamberg, *Doris Lessing Newsletter*, 8, no. 2 (Fall, 1984), 15.

34. Quotation from Doris Lessing in blurb of *The Memoirs of a Survivor*.

35. Roberta Rubenstein, *The Novelistic Vision of Doris Lessing*, p. 240.

36. See Claire Sprague, 'Naming in Marriages: Another View', *Doris Lessing Newsletter*, 7, no. 1 (Summer 1983), 13.

37. Lorna Sage, 'The Available Space', in *Women's Writing: A Challenge to Theory*, ed. Moira Monteith (Brighton: The Harvester Press, 1986), pp. 15–33.

38. Doris Lessing, interview with Christopher Bigsby in *The Radical Imagination and the Liberal Tradition: Interviews with English and American Novelists* by Heide Ziegler and Christopher Bigsby (London: Junction Books, 1982), pp. 188–208.

39. Ibid.

40. Apsley Cherry-Garrard, *The Worst Journey in the World* (London: Chatto and Windus, 1913). Quoted by Doris Lessing in the Afterword to *The Making of the Representative for Planet 8*, pp. 162–90.

41. Judith Stitzel, review of *Documents Relating to the Sentimental Agents in the Volyen Empire* in *Doris Lessing Newsletter*, 7, no. 2 (Winter 1983), 9–10 in which she quotes from Lesley Hazelton, 'Doris Lessing on Feminism, Communism and "space fiction"', *The New York Times Magazine*, 25 July 1982, p. 29.

42. See, for example, Judith Stitzel's review (above), p. 10.

43. Doris Lessing, 'Sufic Searches', *The Literary Review*, no. 49 (July 1982), 10–11.

44. Jonathan Yardley, 'Lessing is More: An "Unknown" author and the Success Syndrome', *Doris Lessing Newsletter*, 9, no. 1 (Spring 1985), 3, 14.

45. Ellen Goodman, 'The Doris Lessing Hoax', *Doris Lessing Newsletter*, 9, no. 1 (Spring 1985), 3.

46. Ibid.

47. 'Doris Lessing Talks about Jane Somers', *Doris Lessing Newsletter*, 10, no. 1 (Spring 1986), 3, 4, 5, 14.

48. Carey Kaplan, review of *The Diaries of Jane Somers*, *Doris Lessing Newsletter*, 10, no. 1 (Spring 1986), 4.

49. 'Doris Lessing Talks about Jane Somers', *Doris Lessing Newsletter*, 10, no. 1 (Spring 1986).

50. Ibid.

51. Carey Kaplan, review of *The Diaries of Jane Somers*, *Doris Lessing Newsletter*, 10, no. 1 (Spring 1986).

52. Lorna Sage, *Doris Lessing*, p. 56.

53. Doris Lessing, 'The Temptation of Jack Orkney' from *The Story of a Non-Marrying Man and Other Stories* (London: Cape, 1972; Harmondsworth, Penguin, 1975).

Select Bibliography

NOTES ON EDITIONS

In this book references are to the Panther (Granada Publishing) editions of
Doris Lessing's novels, except for the following: *Retreat to Innocence*, Michael
Joseph; *The Summer Before the Dark*, Penguin Books; *The Memoirs of a Survivor*,
Picador (Pan Books); *The Diaries of Jane Somers*, Penguin Books and *The Good
Terrorist*, Jonathan Cape. Place of publication is London unless otherwise
indicated.

WORKS BY DORIS LESSING

Novels

The Grass is Singing (1950; New York, 1950)
Children of Violence
   Martha Quest (1952; New York, 1964)
   A Proper Marriage (1954; New York, 1964)
   A Ripple from the Storm (1958; New York, 1966)
   Landlocked (1965; New York, 1966)
   The Four-Gated City (1969; New York, 1969)
Retreat to Innocence (1956; New York, 1957)
The Golden Notebook (1962; New York, 1962)
Briefing for a Descent into Hell (1971; New York, 1971)
The Summer before the Dark (1973; New York, 1973)
The Memoirs of a Survivor (1974; New York, 1975)
Canopus in Argos: Archives
   Re: Colonized Planet 5, Shikasta (1979; New York, 1979)
   The Marriages Between Zones Three, Four, and Five (1980); New York, 1980)
   The Sirian Experiments (1981, New York, 1981)
   The Making of the Representative for Planet 8 (1982; New York, 1982)
   Documents relating to The Sentimental Agents in the Volyen Empire (1983; New
     York, 1983)
The Diaries of Jane Somers (1984; New York 1983, 1984)
The Good Terrorist (1985; New York, 1985)

Short Stories

This Was the Old Chief's Country (1951; New York, 1952)
Five (1953)
The Habit of Loving (1957; New York, 1957)
A Man and Two Women (1963; New York, 1963)
African Stories (1964; New York, 1965)
The Story of a Non-Marrying Man and Other Stories (1972) Published as *The Temptation of Jack Orkney and Other Stories* (New York, 1972)
This Was the Old Chief's Country: Collected African Stories, vol. 1 (1973)
The Sun Between Their Feet: Collected African Stories, vol. 2 (1973)
Two Room Nineteen: Collected Stories, vol. 1 (1978)
The Temptation of Jack Orkney: Collected Stories, vol. 2 (1978)

Plays

Each His Own Wilderness. In *New English Dramatists: Three Plays*, ed. E. Martin Browne (1959)
Play With a Tiger (1962). Also in *Plays by and About Women*, ed. Victoria Sullivan and James Hatch (New York, 1973)

Poems

Fourteen Poems (Northwood, Middlesex, 1959)

Non-fiction

Going Home (1957, revised edn, Panther, 1968; New York, 1968)
In Pursuit of the English: A Documentary (1960; New York, 1961)
Particularly Cats (1967; New York, 1967)
The Wind Blows Away our Words (Pan Books, 1987)
Prisons We Choose to Live Inside (Cape, 1987)

Selected Interviews

Eve Bertelsen, 'The Persistent Personal Voice: Lessing on Rhodesia and Marxism', excerpts from an interview with Doris Lessing, London, 9 January 1984. *Doris Lessing Newsletter*, 9, no. 2 (Fall 1985)
Christopher Bigsby, interview with Doris Lessing in *The Radical Imagination and the Liberal Tradition* by Heide Ziegler and Christopher Bigsby (1982)
C. J. Driver, 'Doris Lessing', an interview in *The New Review*, 1, no. 8 (November 1974), 17–23
Schleuter, Paul (ed.), *A Small Personal Voice* (New York, 1975). Contains interviews with Doris Lessing by Florence Howe, Roy Newquist and Jonah Raskin

Selected Criticism

Draine, Betsy, *Substance Under Pressure: Artistic Coherence and Evolving Form in the Novels of Doris Lessing* (Madison: Univ. of Wisconsin Press, 1983)
Fishburn, Katherine, *The Unexpected Universe of Doris Lessing: A Study in Narrative Technique* (Westport: Greenwood Press, 1985)

Pratt, A. and Dembo, L. S. (eds), *Doris Lessing: Critical Studies* (Madison: Univ. of Wisconsin Press, 1974)

Rubenstein, Roberta, *The Novelistic Vision of Doris Lessing: Breaking the Forms of Consciousness* (Urbana: Univ. of Illinois Press, 1979)

Sage, Lorna, *Doris Lessing* (London: Methuen, 1983)

Singleton, Mary Ann, *The City and the Veld: The Fiction of Doris Lessing* (Lewisburg: Bucknell Univ. Press, 1977)

Sprague, Claire and Tiger, Virginia (eds), *Critical Essays on Doris Lessing* (Boston: G. K. Hall, 1986)

Taylor, Jenny, (ed.), *Notebooks/Memoirs/Archives: Reading and Rereading Doris Lessing* (1982)

Thorpe, Michael, *Doris Lessing's Africa* (London: Evans, 1978)

Journal

Doris Lessing Newsletter, ed. Claire Sprague and published by the Brooklyn College Press, The City University of New York.

Index